Provided
through the generosity of
Indianapolis Power & Light Company
Indiana Historical Society Press

CAMP MORTON 1861-1865

INDIANAPOLIS PRISON CAMP

By

HATTIE LOU WINSLOW

and

JOSEPH R. H. MOORE

INDIANAPOLIS

INDIANA HISTORICAL SOCIETY

1995

Originally published in 1940 as volume 13, number 3 of
the Indiana Historical Society *Publications*

Printed in the United States of America

The paper in this publication meets the minimum requirements of American National
Standard for Information Sciences—Permanence of Paper for Printed Library Materials,
ANSI Z39.48-1984. ∞

Library of Congress Cataloging-in-Publication Data
Winslow, Hattie Lou.
Camp Morton, 1861-1865: Indianapolis prison camp/by Hattie Lou Winslow and
Joseph R.H. Moore.
p. cm.
Includes bibliographical references and index.
ISBN 0-87195-114-2 (cloth)
1. Camp Morton (Ind.) 2. Indianapolis (Ind.)—History—Civil War, 1861-1865—Prison-
ers and prisons. 3. United States—History—Civil War, 1861-1865—Prisoners and pris-
ons. I. Moore, Joseph R. H. II. Title.
E616.M8W56 1995
973.7′72—dc20   95-19588
                                                                                  CIP

ACKNOWLEDGMENTS

THE AUTHORS must express their thanks to Dr. Coleman, to Miss Armstrong, to their coadjutors at the Historical Bureau and State Library, and to the many friends who have by their suggestions increased the human interest of this small part of the story of the War between the States. During a work covering some years, it is very evident that such credit as may accrue is due to a great many people, so many that were it not for the "friendliness of the folk" such a work could not come even to moderate completion.

FOREWORD

AT THE Indiana History Conference in December, 1932, Joseph R. H. Moore, head of the social studies department of Emmerich Manual Training High School, Indianapolis, read a paper upon the Civil War prisoners' depot at Camp Morton, in which he had long been interested. He generously agreed to extend his study as he had time and opportunity, and present it to the Indiana Historical Society for publication. Meanwhile, Mrs. Hattie Lou Winslow, of the social studies department of Shortridge High School, Indianapolis, also became interested in Camp Morton and prepared a history of it in connection with her work at Butler University. Mr. Moore and Mrs. Winslow thereafter combined their materials for this publication.

The many purposes served by Camp Morton—recruiting camp, prison for Confederate soldiers, and place of detention for Union soldiers on parole—entitle it to a place in Civil War annals. At various times there has been controversy over the treatment and condition of the prisoners kept at Camp Morton. The authors have attempted to give a fair and objective treatment of the subject, and to provide an honest picture of the life of the camp.

CHRISTOPHER B. COLEMAN
Secretary Indiana Historical Society

CONTENTS

ILLUSTRATIONS

I. TRAINING CAMP, 1861

During the 1850's every good citizen of Indianapolis knew very well the tract of land now circumscribed by Nineteenth Street, Talbott Avenue, Twenty-second Street, and Central Avenue. It contained approximately thirty-six acres and belonged to Samuel Henderson. One hundred years ago the city had begun pushing slowly out along East Washington Street. The south side was already well settled—with some fine dwellings—but the north side was just beginning to branch out as a social entity. A few houses were to be found north of Washington Street; further north were farms and orchards, and away out in the country was the Asylum for the Blind. There were no houses on Illinois Street north of Ninth Street, and east of Illinois there were no more thoroughfares until a winding country road was reached, the predecessor of our present Central Avenue. For four blocks south of Nineteenth Street there was not even a farmhouse, nothing but fields and an occasional orchard.

The Honorable Samuel Henderson—he became the first mayor of Indianapolis in 1846—owned a large farm in this region, and the thirty-six acres formed the crown of the farm, both by reason of its height and because it was the most beautiful part of his property. It was partially wooded with scattered hardwoods, mostly black walnut and oak, with fine greensward between the groves. There were at least four good springs on the area, and since Mr. Henderson was known to be friendly to everyone, it became the favorite place for "twosomes," for family picnics, and, when the Methodists felt the need, it was the logical place for a camp meeting.

On Illinois Street, Twenty-second Street marked the northern limit of civilization. Beyond was a wilderness, perhaps because in that area a tract of low, soft ground through which ran a "bayou" put a stop to traffic. Northeast of the city, about three miles from "the Governor's Circle" was "the swamp," drained by two more bayous. One of these became Pogue's Run as it went south and southwest; the other, running

1

somewhat south of west, cut across the eastern end of Henderson's Grove, flowed west about the northerly line of Nineteenth Street until it passed a little west of Alabama Street, then northwesterly to Twenty-second Street, where it turned west again before emptying into Fall Creek.

This creek was usually dry in the summer, but at the time of the spring rains it became a turbulent stream, overflowing its banks and doing damage all out of proportion to its size. During the legislative session of 1837, commissioners were appointed to study the situation and to construct a ditch large and deep enough to accommodate the water of this small stream.[1] The work consisted mainly of straightening and deepening the existing bed to allow better flowage and thus do away with the occasional stagnant places which in summer became evil-smelling mudholes and breeding places for the mosquito. This improvement was called the "State Ditch," and later, by the prisoners of Camp Morton, the "Potomac."

Toward the end of the 1850's there began to be talk about utilizing the area known as Henderson's or Otis' Grove as a site for the State Fairground; it was not too near the settled part of the city, but near enough to be reached conveniently in the days when people thought nothing of walking a mile and a half and back again. In 1859 possession was actually taken, and certain structures were built to fulfill the requirements for "a place of universal interest." Along the northern side of the grounds was a long structure like a shed. It had a strong roof with suitable uprights, and not much in the way of siding— wide boards placed vertically, with battens covering the cracks. Some of the boards seem to have been green, or perhaps the nails that were supposed to hold the battens were not driven in straight; at any rate, there was much criticism because the horses stabled in these long sheds were not properly protected, especially where the south side of the structure was left open

[1]The act appointed Calvin Fletcher and Thomas Johnson commissioners "to superintend the draining of the swamps and low lands immediately north east of Indianapolis, the out let of which over flows the grounds west, north east, and north of the State house square." *Laws of Indiana,* 1836-37 (local), pp. 409-10; Ignatius Brown, "History of Indianapolis, from 1818 to 1868," in *Logan's Indianapolis Directory* . . . (Indianapolis, Logan & Co., 1868), pp. 39-40.

2

to the weather. At the west end of the grounds were 250 stalls for cattle, with sheds for the prize sheep and hogs, all well covered. In addition there was a hall for the exhibition of farm machinery, domestic manufactures, and farm produce. Near the east end was a large dining room, and about the center of the grounds was the only two-story building in the place, an office building with several sizeable rooms.[2] By 1861 Henderson's Grove or the State Fairgrounds was well known all over the state.

On April 12 of that year Fort Sumter was fired upon. There was intense excitement on the streets of Indianapolis. Little business was done in the stores, but a great deal of talking went on in the streets. Did the sovereign state of South Carolina have the right to fire on the flag of the United States? Was Anderson right in defying the governor and state? There had never in the history of the city been a day like this one.[3] A mass meeting at the Marion County Courthouse had to be adjourned to the Metropolitan Theater, and this, in turn, overflowed to the Masonic Hall across the street. Two days later, when word came of President Lincoln's proclamation asking for seventy-five thousand volunteers, Governor Oliver Perry Morton stepped forward on the stage. Morton came from a race of fighters; he was named for a great American fighter. Far from being a "yes" man, he might have been described as a "no compromise" man, for he believed that the recalcitrant South should be compelled to live up to the terms of the Constitution of the United States. Without a day's delay he telegraphed the President an offer of ten thousand men. Recruiting stations were opened that day, and members of military companies and other volunteers rushed to enlist.

On the same day Morton chose his adjutant general—a fellow lawyer who had had experience in the army, whose judgment he trusted, and whose loyalty to the Constitution was

[2]James Sutherland (comp.), *Indianapolis Directory and Business Mirror for 1861* . . . (Indianapolis: Bowen, Stewart & Co., 1861), pp. 47-49. The description of the grounds is accompanied by a chart showing the location of the various points of interest. See also State Board of Agriculture, *Report,* 1859 (Indianapolis, 1861), pp. lxvii, lxxx, lxxxi.

[3]See John H. Holliday's account of these days in Jacob Piatt Dunn's *Greater Indianapolis* . . . (2 volumes, Chicago, 1910), I, 217 ff.

beyond doubt. General Wallace, known to us as "Lew" Wallace, came to Indianapolis to survey the town with the Governor in search of a suitable spot for the reception of the Indiana troops as they came in. An area extending west from the State House toward the river received some consideration, but it was hardly large enough and there were no suitable buildings. Henderson's Grove had all the requisites. It was far enough out of town; it had water, shade, and buildings; it was on as high ground as there was in the neighborhood; and, best of all, it had happy connections in the minds of the people.

On April 17, the first troops came into camp. They were, of course, the local companies of Guards and Zouaves, but men and boys from further out in the state came in from day to day and were formed into companies and regiments as fast as they assembled. These first regiments of Indiana soldiers were well drilled and well uniformed. They were fine specimens physically, too.

The practical problems of a training camp were many. Where to put the new soldiers? How to feed them? How to control them? How to train them in military tactics? The existing buildings were utilized as offices. The office near the carriage entrance was made headquarters, with Colonel Joseph J. Reynolds in charge; the first floor of the committee building became the quartermaster's office; the second floor was the medical inspector's office under Dr. John S. Bobbs; in the large dining hall was the commissary's store, where food was dispensed on the requisition of company officers; the treasurer's office became the guardhouse; and the power hall was fitted up as a hospital.

The remaining halls on the grounds were fitted with bunks, but as they could not accommodate more than two thousand men, the long rows of stalls were put to use as hunters' camps, one side open to the weather. Six men were assigned to each stall, their cooking fire out in front. Signs became the fashion, and such men as had artistic instinct, and some who did not, put up their modest advertisements: "Bates House," "Burnett House," "washing and ironing," "dress making," "hair dressing," and the like. Across the east end of the area sprang up another row of sheds, also open to the weather, and along the south edge of the camp as near as might be to the State Ditch, other rows of stalls were erected.[4] By the end of April, 1861, there were shelters of a sort for six thousand men.

The new sheds were built of green lumber, the boards ten to twelve inches wide, and battens four inches wide. Sun and rain got in their work on the green lumber, and soon the soldiers were complaining heartily about their drafty, leaking quarters.[5] Some of the new "stalls" were closed on all four sides, and their inside arrangement was thought to be very good. Along two sides of the shed, extending seven feet toward the middle, were constructed four tiers of bunks. The lowest tier was one foot from the ground, which served as a floor; it was three feet to the second, and three feet to the third, which was on the level of the eaves. Two feet of space were allowed each man. With this arrangement each barracks would hold about 320 men. There was space enough between the two rows of bunks for long tables, serving as dining tables and as a suitable place for playing games. Entrance was through large "barn doors" at each end, where the floor became a mudhole at every heavy rainstorm, although the outside was ditched to carry off the rain.[6] The camp was surrounded by a high board fence, with armed guards every twenty paces.[7]

Confusion was inevitable in a camp so hastily put into operation, and so soon overflowing with its thousands of newly enlisted men. Some of the men were sworn in at the State House and sent to Camp Morton for regular muster and placement, while other groups went directly to the camp. Muster rolls were badly written. Many of the men were illiterate, and the company clerks who wrote their names often misspelled them. Many recruits thought it was a joke to give a ridiculous name, while others, who had run away from home, gave false names in order "not to be catched."

[4]Indianapolis *Sentinel*, April 23, 1861, p. 3, c. 2.

[5]John A. Wyeth, "Cold Cheer at Camp Morton," in *Century Magazine*, XLI, 846 (April, 1891).

[6]*Ibid.;* John A. Wyeth, *With Sabre and Scalpel* (Harper & Brothers, New York and London, 1914), pp. 288-89.

[7]Letter of Herman Bamberger, dated April 21, 1861, in Indianapolis *News*, May 18, 1914, p. 10, c. 1.

As the troops kept pouring in, it became necessary to supplement the barracks and stalls with tents, and then to divide the troops and give them quarters outside the camp, although Camp Morton remained the principal station. The Zouave Regiment, or Eleventh Indiana, of special interest because of its famous colonel, Lew Wallace, who had resigned his position as adjutant, was moved to the old Bellefontaine car shop.[8]

Two Irish regiments and a German regiment were formed, since it was found wise not to mix nationalities. Experience later proved that it was not wise to use a German regiment and an Irish regiment side by side in a charge, lest their ardor to see which could "git thar fust" upset a carefully planned military maneuver. Both groups loved music, and their rivalry in singing gave other regiments many a fine evening's entertainment. There were also a railroad regiment and a mechanic's regiment.[9]

When the cold weather set in, the members of this latter, under Colonel A. D. Streight, conceived the idea of warming their tents by constructing a series of hot-air furnaces. Beneath each tent was dug a trench some feet longer than the diameter of the tent and covered first with stone, and then with earth. At one end a huge square hole served as a furnace mouth and the smoke, escaping through a chimney at the other end, warmed the earth. This arrangement left the tent clear of smoke with no danger of fire.[10]

When Camp Morton was first occupied, an attempt was made to confine all drills to the grounds, but it soon became apparent that the buildings and numerous trees permitted nothing more than squad and company drills. An area just south of the camp was then acquired, where large bodies of troops could be taught to good advantage. Over this drill ground, where officers and men alike were struggling to take on a military cast, there occasionally rang out an order more notable for its urgency than for its conformity to soldierly usages. One captain who had been a railroader for years saw his

[8]Indianapolis *Sentinel*, April 26, 1861, p. 3, c. 3; Indianapolis *Journal*, April 25, 1861, p. 2, c. 1.

[9]Indianapolis *Sentinel*, September 7, 1861, p. 3, c. 2.

[10]Indianapolis *Journal*, November 22, 1861, p. 3, c. 1.

command about to march into a fence. "Down brakes!" he shouted. "Down brakes!" Another officer allowed his attention to wander for a moment during regimental drill; suddenly he realized that the command to halt had been given and in his excitement betrayed how recently he had come from the farm by resorting to the old familiar "whoa!"[11]

Camp Morton quickly became a center of attraction. Roads leading to it were filled with vehicles of all sorts, private and public. It was fashionable to drive out to Camp Morton, and in the afternoon the carriages of the best people of the town might be seen appearing and disappearing in the clouds of dust that hovered over the most respectable roads. The hack business became a thriving enterprise. Ten cents was the fare from the Circle, the "prop" paying a city license fee of ten dollars a year for the use of the street to and from the camp.[12]

Sunday was the popular day for visitors. On April 21, 1861, it was estimated that there were ten thousand of them, making, with the five thousand soldiers at camp, a huge throng for those times.[13] These visitors did not understand that much of the work of an army camp must proceed on Sunday as well as on week days, nor did they grasp the fact that homesick boys must be kept occupied at all times. There was little to set apart the Sabbath day save that at times religious services were held for the different groups. Everyday labor went on as usual among the three hundred civilians about the camp, and the speakers had to compete with the sound of sawing and hammering, with teamsters addressing mules in the language which they seemed best to understand; with the shrill noises of nails being drawn from boxes; and with drill sergeants addressing their squads of recruits.[14]

The Sunday following the deluge of visitors, the camp was ordered closed to all outsiders. "The camp has been so crowded since it was formed," stated the *Sentinel* of April 27, "that it is only a matter of justice to the men to allow them

[11]Indianapolis *Sentinel*, November 4, 1861, p. 3, c. 2.

[12]Indianapolis *Journal*, April 24, 1861, p. 3, c. 2; July 13, p. 3, c. 1.

[13]Letter of Herman Bamberger, dated April 21, 1861, in Indianapolis *News*, May 18, 1914, p. 10, c. 1.

[14]Indianapolis *Journal*, April 22, 1861, p. 3, c. 1.

one day in the week free from intrusion, to say nothing of the respect due to the day."

During that week a barrack rumor did its best to mortify all good citizens. It was noised abroad that the Honorable Stephen A. Douglas would speak at Camp Morton. The city hummed with excitement. The state legislators, then in special session, marched out to the camp in a body, preceded by the National Guard Band. Such a jam resulted that Mr. Douglas could not even see the camp, much less inspect it. And there was no speech. Douglas was finally obliged to escape by a side road to rejoin his party.[15] In the meantime a report went out among the crowd that the wells had been poisoned and that a peddler had been selling poisoned oranges in camp. To still the first report, the guard at the wells was doubled, and the second was disposed of by the quick wit of Dr. Fletcher, who stopped a riot by eating one of the libeled oranges.[16] These matters resulted in a tightening of discipline and a more military atmosphere.

The government regulations gave the bugle calls for the day as follows:[17]

1. Reveille .... 6 A. M.	7. Dinner ....12½ M.
2. Police call .... 6¼ A. M.	8. Drill .... 2 P. M.
3. Breakfast .... 7 A. M.	9. Retreat Parade ..... 5 P. M.
4. Guard Mounting .... 8 A. M.	10. Supper .... 6 P. M.
5. Drill .... 8½ A. M.	11. Tattoo .... 9 P. M.
6. Drill ....11 A. M.	12. Taps ....10 P. M.

Distribution of soldiers' mail became a problem as soon as the camp was established. Before the end of April, 1861, J. F. Dougherty was made a "route agent" between the town and the camp. Letters and papers were sent to company headquarters four times a day, and by May 1 there were about two hundred letters in and out each day. On May 4, a new post office was commissioned at the camp (Dillard C. Donohue, postmaster) so that mail could be sent direct.[18]

[15]Indianapolis *Journal*, April 25, 1861, p. 3, c. 1; Indianapolis *Sentinel*, April 25, 1861, p. 3, c. 2.

[16]Indianapolis *Journal*, April 25, 1861, p. 3, c. 1; Indianapolis *Sentinel*, April 25, 1861, p. 3, c. 1.

[17]Indianapolis *Journal*, extra, April 21, 1861, c. 4.

[18]*Ibid.*, May 10, 1861, p. 3, c. 2; Post Office Index, Indiana Division, Indiana State Library.

Soldier recreation was plentiful. Games brought from home included checkers, chess, and card games, and there was the usual "rough stuff" such as the Knights of Malta initiation—this meant being tossed on a piece of tent canvas handled by a squad of tormentors.[19] There were always rumors about the progress of the war, interlarded with stories of blunders made by officers and men. These, it was admitted, improved directly as the square of the distance they traveled. Some one officer or enlisted man was likely to serve as the camp "butt." Captain Will C. Moreau, a relative of the victor of Hohenlinden, was one of these. While in Indiana to recruit a company of cavalry, he gave a dinner for his friends and several prominent citizens. Instead of the "beans, salt pork and sheet iron biscuit" which usually comprised the dinner at an officer's headquarters, the *Journal* describes Captain Moreau's feast as "a dinner, which in the way of oysters, champagne, and all the most desirable additions of a recherche feast, has had no parallel in our memory." Such an occasion caused no end of comment around the camp.[20]

One of the most active agencies in helping with the emergency was the Ladies Patriotic Association, organized by Mrs. Morton and conducted by her for both Union recruits and Confederate prisoners. She was a militant president, and when she thought that the work was not up to the necessities of the moment, she scolded the members publicly through the columns of the *Journal* and *Sentinel*. The association was nonsectarian, nonpolitical, and as a rule very active, often meeting at the Governor's Mansion. One Saturday the group made over two hundred dollars worth of flannel into garments.[21] Havelocks were made for the men, and when an epidemic of measles brought a sudden demand, sheets, pillowcases, towels, and shirts were provided.[22]

These ladies also conducted campaigns for gifts for the camp. On October 10, Governor Morton sent out a special appeal to the ladies for blankets, socks, gloves and mittens,

[19]Indianapolis *Journal*, May 25, 1861, p. 3, c. 1.
[20]*Ibid.*, October 22, 1861, p. 3, c. 2.
[21]*Ibid.*, April 21, 1861, extra, c. 3.
[22]*Ibid.*, May 17, 1861, p. 3, c. 1.

woolen shirts, and drawers. Six weeks later it was announced that tons of materials had been received, enough of everything except gloves and mittens.[23] Other appeals, made to patriotic societies throughout the state, met with a most generous response. Articles most acceptable were "beef or salt pork, flour, sugar and rice, in barrels or sacks; white beans, dried apples and peaches, in barrels or sacks; crackers in barrels; hard soap, tallow or star candles, in boxes; bacon—either hams, shoulders or sides, in barrels, casks or boxes."[24]

The problem of clothing was for many months a serious one. The boys often came to camp barefoot and with clothes for warm weather only. Many had not much more than trousers and shirt. Pending the arrival of government uniforms and supplies, the state had to do its best, aided by gifts. Two regiments were clothed in cadet satinet, two-piece suits, at $7.90 each. One regiment had jean uniforms at $6.50 each; another, a better grade of the same material, at $7.50 a suit. The Fifth Indiana wore gray satinet at $6.75 a uniform, while the gay Zouaves rejoiced in ten-dollar costumes of the Josephian variety. Flannel shirts cost $1.40 each, hats $1.25, and shoes $1.15 a pair. By the time cold weather approached, it had to be admitted that the war would not be over in a few weeks, and officials began to demand that jackets and trousers should be all wool.[25]

During the first summer the health of the soldiers at Camp Morton was remarkably good, giving little warning of the terrible health problems of the later years. Drs. John M. Kitchen and Patrick H. Jameson were in charge of the sick among the troops at the camp, and were asked to provide suitable hospital accommodations. Sick calls in the morning regularly brought all minor cases to the receiving hospital on the camp grounds, while serious cases were sent by ambulance to the City Hospital, a new building not heretofore occupied. It became an army hospital on April 29.[26] In May, 1861,

[23]Holliday, "Civil War Times," in Dunn, *Greater Indianapolis*, I, 224.

[24]Indianapolis *Sentinel*, April 22, 1861, p. 2, c. 3.

[25]Holliday, "Civil War Times," in Dunn, *Greater Indianapolis*, I, 222.

[26]*Report of Hospital Surgeons, Drs. Kitchen & Jameson* (Indianapolis, 1863), in *Indiana and the War*, I, No. 31, Indiana Division, Indiana State Library; Indianapolis *Sentinel*, August 16, 1861, p. 3, c. 4.

out of probably seven thousand men in camp, there were only fifteen hospital cases, with about one hundred and fifty temporary cases suffering from diarrhea or colds.[27] When the first death occurred at Camp Morton, the members of the legislature made personal contributions for the purchase of a lot in which soldiers dying in camp might be buried if there were no relatives to claim the body.[28]

Of all the problems at Camp Morton in 1861, the most constantly annoying one was the food question. Complaining about the food was the standard amusement of the soldiers, indoor and outdoor. All good soldiers complain about everything, the complaints, like water, flowing downward, for no wise soldier complains so that his superior officers can hear. It must be remembered that no one knew very much about dietary requirements or about how to secure in quantity the multitudinous things that a large camp needs. There was a very limited variety of canned goods. Salt meat of varying degrees of saltiness, salt fish, fruit and vegetables, and jelly, were about all these boys of 1861 could hope for. "Glassed" fruit was expensive, largely on account of the price of sugar, and the boxes from home too often resulted in intestinal disturbances of a serious character. There was no market of foods on an enormous scale, as there is now. The wonder is that rations were not infinitely worse.

The first commissary general was Isaiah Mansur, an honest man and a hard worker. As it happened, he had to begin the feeding of the troops and, simultaneously, learn all the army rules and regulations concerning supplies. No provisions were on hand and he had to buy where he could and in small quantities. Since a large proportion of the boys came from homes where food was plentiful, and since they were all unacquainted with army cooking and camp economy, the Governor and Mr. Mansur thought it wise to issue larger allotments of food than the regular army allowance granted. The following table will show how advantageous the arrangement was for the troops:[29]

[27]Indianapolis *Journal*, May 1, 1861, p. 3, c. 2.
[28]*Ibid.*, May 3, 1861, p. 3, c. 3.
[29]Indiana *House Journal*, 1861 (special session), pp. 213-14.

ARMY RATIONS PER COMPANY			RATIONS ISSUED BY MR. MANSUR
Pork	75	lbs.	110 lbs.
or			
Beef	125	lbs.	150 lbs.
Flour	112⅔	lbs.	150 lbs.
or			
Hard Bread	100	lbs.	none
Beans	8	qts.	130 lbs.
or			
Rice	10	lbs.	12 lbs.
Coffee	6	lbs.	8 lbs.
Sugar	12	lbs.	16 lbs.
Vinegar	1	gal.	2½ gals.
Candles	1½	lbs.	3 lbs.
Soap	4	lbs.	6 lbs.
Salt	2	qts.	12 lbs.
		Potatoes	100 lbs.
		Pepper	1 lb.
		Dried fruit	1½ lbs.
		Onions	3 bu.
		Pickles and other anti-	
		scorbutics	no special amount

Nevertheless, the complaints poured into the newspapers. The meat was too salty, the dried apples wormy, the beans unsound, and, most loudly criticized of all, the coffee was adulterated with parched beans. Many of these boys had been accustomed in their own homes to coffee substitutes made of parched grains including chicory, rye, and maize. "Rye-'n'Injun" made a hot drink that was good and relatively harmless (at least, no one needed to worry about caffeine or theobromine, while knowledge of vitamins and calories were at least two generations in the future); the troops were not hungry (it was no uncommon thing to see soldiers pelting each other with potatoes or bacon or loaves of bread);[30] but the citizens of Indiana were vastly excited. There was talk of unlawful profits in the Commissary General's office, and much sentimental indignation over the injustice done to Indiana's heroic sons. To think "that the poor boys should be put off with anything less than the fat of the land afforded!" There began an inpouring of boxes from home: roast fowl,

[30]Terrell, *Report*, I, 452.

baked ham, fresh butter and eggs, jellies, accompanied too often by pound cake, pickles, and other indigestible goodies that were regarded without charity by the surgeons at the emergency hospital.

The legislature insisted upon an investigation of the Commissary General's office. The report of the investigating committee exonerated Mansur; in fact, it served to show how good a job had been done under the worst possible conditions, and that Mansur had lost personally instead of making large sums unlawfully. The only proof of trouble had to do with the way the coffee was handled before it reached Mr. Mansur's hands, a matter for which he was in no way responsible. Spoiled meat had been served on one day, but it had been replaced with good meat as soon as the trouble was reported. Financial records were in very good shape considering the fact that a large business had been done by inexperienced persons. The Senate took no action, but the House, of a political cast disinclined to support Mansur, passed a resolution demanding his removal. As Mr. Mansur had accepted the position only out of a sense of duty, he took this opportunity to resign.[31]

Governor Morton appointed Asahel Stone to take Mansur's place. Like his predecessor, Stone furnished many items not provided for by army regulations. For a few months things went better, but presently there was a complaint that the coffee was not only adulterated, but "the worst on the market." In the fall of 1861 the United States Government took over all the work of subsisting the troops in Indiana during their training period. From that time on standard army rations were given out, and the boys began to realize how well Mansur and Stone had looked after them.[32] At least under the new regime they were broken in before they went into the field.

Constant turnover of the higher officers was another characteristic of the camp at this early time. Since no good officer wanted to stay in camp doing the work of a nursery maid when there was fighting to be done elsewhere, there was

[31]Terrell, *Report*, I, 451-54; Indiana *House Journal*, 1861 (special session), pp. 213-18, 242-43, 253-54; Indiana *Senate Journal*, 1861 (special session), p. 164.

[32]Terrell, *op. cit.*, I, 454-55.

a succession of resignations among the higher officers who left to go into the field. Replacements had to be made from officers more or less new to the work. Practically all the more important men connected with Camp Morton were criticized bitterly in letters that were sent home from camp.

Clothing supplies were constantly under criticism, especially after cold weather set in, for a large part of them, purchased at the price of first-grade wool, were said to be shoddy. Men's minds were full of worry and tempers were short. After the United States took control, Major Alexander Montgomery, United States Quartermaster at Indianapolis, became involved in a controversy with Governor Morton and the rest of the state government over the purchase of overcoats for troops in the field, and the resulting delay caused serious discomfort to the poor boys who were forced to do without the coats during the wrangling. The overcoat was the most expensive part of a soldier's equipment, and both lack of materials and inefficiency in turning them out were of serious consequence to both soldiers and prisoners.[38]

Governor Morton probably considered his cup of trouble full with these problems, but others were soon added. Recurring scandals, attempts to run the guards, and difficulties with inefficient officers kept him busy. The first six regiments were completed, started for the field, returned, were discharged and re-enlisted. New men were constantly being taken into the training units, when in February, 1862, a new and imperative need appeared in the troubled field of military activities. Prisoners of war were being taken in large numbers, and had to be taken care of. Prison camps were scattered all over the northern states, wherever transportation facilities and local conditions made it possible to care for large groups of men. Camp Morton met the requirements better than many places and was taken over by the Federal Government to house Confederate prisoners.

[38]Indianapolis *Journal*, October 8, 1861, p. 2, c. 1 ; Indianapolis *Sentinel*, November 5, 1861, p. 2, c. 2-3 ; November 6, 1861, p. 2, c. 1, 2 ; Terrell, *Report*, I, 316-18.

II. PRISONERS' CAMP UNDER
RICHARD OWEN, 1862

IN THE early days of the Civil War, neither the North nor the South had any organization for handling prisoners. Both sides expected the war to be of short duration, and for some time no attempt was made to detain captured soldiers. They were paroled on oath not to serve in the field as combatants until duly exchanged, and then turned loose to make their way home as best they could. Such a plan was humane and efficient in minor conflicts, but when it was realized that a long struggle was inevitable, provision for the confinement of prisoners became necessary.

By law and army regulations this duty fell to the Quartermaster General, Montgomery C. Meigs. The regulations called for a commissary general of prisoners who was to keep an account of the prisoners, assume charge of all captives taken by his government, manage the business of exchange in case of cartel, and transmit to the prisoners held by the enemy such supplies as were sent them. Accordingly, General Meigs, in July, 1861, asked Secretary of War Simon Cameron to appoint such an officer. This appointment, delayed until October of that year, fell to Lieutenant Colonel William H. Hoffman, of the Eighth Infantry, still on parole from General David E. Twiggs' surrender of the Texas garrison.[1] Hoffman gathered around him a small group of hand-picked men through whose efforts a system of prison camps was gradually worked out.

There were at least three groups of men who came under the designation of prisoners of war. First there were the political prisoners. In the fall of 1861, a system of passports was introduced in the North, and in July, 1862, it seemed

[1]For a general discussion of the prison situation in 1861-62, see William Best Hesseltine, *Civil War Prisons: A Study in War Psychology* (Ohio State University Press, Columbus, 1930), pp. 34 ff.; for Hoffman's appointment, see also *The War of the Rebellion: A Compilation of the Official Records of the Union and Confederate Armies,* cited hereafter as *Official Records,* 2 series (8 volumes. Washington, D. C., 1894-1899), III, 48, 121.

necessary to suspend the writ of habeas corpus. Thousands of persons were "arrested on suspicion," and could be held in prison without trial for an indefinite period. All of our generation is well acquainted with war hysteria. Men and women were arrested on the most absurd charges, some because they "looked, funny," some because of poor eyesight, some because of peculiarities of speech, some because they had what was supposed to be "a southern accent." There were thousands of these unfortunates, victims of "a little brief authority" in the wrong hands. These people as a rule had no recourse, and since they could not be held in the ordinary prisons, some place had to be found where they could be retained until the hysteria died.

Second came the officers of the Confederate Army— gentlemen accustomed to the life of gentlemen, used to personal attendance, good horses, and such pleasures as the times furnished. Such men might easily endure the hardships of military life in the field, but the manifold discomforts of a prison camp, together with a constantly growing sense of futility, made them utterly miserable and easy prey to disease.

The third and much the largest group consisted of the noncommissioned officers and men. As a group they were without the mental and moral resources of the officers, although physically they could better withstand the hardships of prison life. Most of them were insufficiently clothed even for summer, and there was never an overcoat among them. The fact that many of them did not have shoes meant the prevalence of hookworm with its attendant troubles. Few of them were uniformed. Homemade garments dyed with the brownish stain of the walnut were so generally worn that the nickname "but'nuts" was almost inevitable.[2] These men suffered from intestinal troubles due to a lack of good food, and they were pediculous to a miserable degree. This condition prevailed in prison camps both North and South, and was one of the causes of the high mortality rate.[3]

Before Hoffman's appointment as commissary general of

[2][Catharine Merrill], *The Soldier of Indiana in the War for the Union* (2 volumes. Indianapolis, Merrill and Company, 1866, 1869), I, 317-18.

[3]Hans Zinsser, *Rats, Lice and History* (Boston, 1935).

prisoners these three groups of prisoners were housed together in the temporary prison camps—with the worst possible results—but in February, 1862, came the demand for prison space on a large scale, and the necessity of segregating different types of prisoners was taken into consideration. This was the first truly cheerful month for the North, with the capture of Fort Henry on the sixth and Fort Donelson on the sixteenth. General Henry W. Halleck sought places where prisoners could be cared for without withdrawing men from the Union forces to guard them. The system finally developed under Hoffman provided that general officers be sent to a small island in Boston Harbor where Fort Warren was located (being desperate villains, they should be securely imprisoned); lesser commissioned officers were sent to Johnson's Island in the harbor of Sandusky, Ohio; and noncommissioned officers and privates were sent to eight scattered camps including Camp Douglas, at Chicago, the largest; Camp Chase at Columbus, Ohio; Camp Butler, at Springfield, Illinois; and Camp Morton, at Indianapolis, the third largest of the group.[4]

After the fall of Fort Donelson, Halleck telegraphed Governor Morton, asking him how many prisoners he could provide for. On February 17 the Governor replied, "We can take 3,000 if necessary," but 3,700 came to be quartered at Camp Morton.[5]

No one had known exactly what to do with the few prisoners in Indianapolis before this date. Sometimes, if they had the means, they were allowed to live at a hotel, reporting to headquarters once a day. Those without money were permitted to get jobs in the town, and use the income for their support. There was an entire lack of regulation with regard to their care; persons responsible for them had simply done whatever was most practicable under the circumstances. To

[4] *Official Records,* 2 series, III, 269, 270-71, 274, 276, 277, 278, 281, 288, 337; Hesseltine, *Civil War Prisons,* p. 41. For pictures of the various camps, hospitals, officials, and prisoners of note, see Holland Thompson (ed.), *Prisons and Hospitals (The Photographic History of The Civil War,* Volume Seven. The Review of Reviews Co., New York, 1911).

[5] *Official Records,* 2 series, III, 269 ff.; Jacob P. Dunn, *Indiana and Indianans . . .* (5 volumes. Chicago and New York, 1919), II, 613-14; Indianapolis *Sentinel,* March 15, 1862, and following issues.

provide for an influx of 3,700 men was a problem to tax the best heads. The doctors of the city threw themselves into the work, and the citizens, touched by the miserable appearance of the captives, gave clothes and bedding, jelly and fresh bread of their own baking.[6]

A stupendous load of charitable work was undertaken by the Sanitary Commission, in a way a forerunner of the Red Cross. At Camp Morton such problems were also taken care of by the ladies of the town who had been organized under the leadership of Mrs. Morton, but here again local conditions interfered with good results. There were so many sympathizers with the Confederate cause in Marion County that many of the ladies with Union sympathies feared that work for the prisoners would put them under suspicion.

Mention should be made at this place of the troubles at some of the other camps, since they throw much light on the happenings at Camp Morton. Fort Warren was a masonry structure on one of the many hundreds of small islands—nothing more than great heaps of gravel—in Boston Harbor, dependent for security on the swift currents that surrounded them at all stages of the tide. No one ever lived through the waters of Shirley Gut, surrounding Deer Island, and while Fort Warren stood on the highest point on Governor's Island and, therefore, had the best position as a lookout, it was also the coldest and the windiest spot in the harbor, and naturally the most difficult to heat. The fireplaces and an occasional stove formed the totally inadequate source of warmth, with fuel often at a premium. Confederate generals suffered extremely from climatic conditions, since they were not accustomed to the chill of a stone structure during a nor'easter, with the mercury at twenty below.

Johnson's Island likewise depended on its situation for the security of the prisoners.[7] There were not, of course, the deep

[6]Holliday, "Civil War Times," in Dunn, *Greater Indianapolis*, I, 226.

[7]For Colonel Hoffman's report to General Meigs on the selection of Johnson's Island and his recommendations concerning the buildings to be erected, see *Official Records*, 2 series, III, 54-57. See also *ibid.*, III, 122-23, 135-36, 326-27; H. Carpenter, "Plain Living at Johnson's Island," in *Century Magazine*, XLI, 705-18 (March, 1891); Joe Barbiere, *Scraps from the Prison Table at Camp Chase and Johnson's Island* (Doylestown, Pa., 1868).

water and the strong current of Boston Harbor, but a mile of water and the mud flats helped a good deal. The Confederate officers who were the inmates of the prison were worth taking some risk to rescue, but no attempt of this sort was ever successfully carried out. Newspaper scares and the outpourings of such reckless talkers as Clement Laird Vallandigham gave warning, and the prison on Johnson's Island was closely guarded at all times. It probably maintained the most severe discipline of all the camps.

Camp Douglas at Chicago had the worst situation of all prisoners' camps in the North.[8] It was on low ground, badly drained, and had no protection from the land winds. Consequently the death rate among the prisoners, who arrived poorly clothed and ill fed, was very great. Due to the strong feeling in the city against the prisoners, relief work among the men was relatively less than elsewhere. There was also dishonesty among the civilian employees, and trouble arising from the type of men placed in charge of the camp. The feeling of helplessness among the prisoners in the face of legal wrongs that they could not right, their poor health and the high death rate, the bad food conditions and lack of hospitalization, all combined to furnish additional proof, if any were needed, of the correctness of General Sherman's famous observation on the nature of war.

The problem of converting Camp Morton into a prisoners' camp fell to Captain James A. Ekin, an assistant quartermaster general of the United States Army who had been stationed at Indianapolis since the preceding August. Strict economy in all changes was demanded by Colonel Hoffman and General Meigs. The stock stalls along the north fence, which had housed Indiana troops during the preceding summer and autumn, were remodeled to provide six apartments for sleeping purposes and one for eating purposes, and additional barracks were erected of lumber that had been used for temporary stables.[9] There was no time to have the work done before the

[8] *Official Records*, 2 series, IV, 106, 110, 111; *Reminiscences of Chicago During the Civil War*, with an introduction by Mabel McIlvaine (R. R. Donnelley & Sons Company, Chicago, 1914), 161-94.

[9] Terrell, *Report*, I, 446, 447, 456; *Official Records*, 2 series, III, 278, 301, 335-36.

arrival of the prisoners, or according to any carefully considered plan.

Colonel Hoffman, having inspected the camp after the prisoners came, made the criticism on March 12, 1862, that the quarters were "dark and close and there must be much sickness . . . unless some improvements are made."[10] Shortly after, prisoners were transferred from one barracks at a time into tents, so that windows could be put in the dark buildings to give more light and air during the warm weather. In June new barracks were erected to relieve the overcrowded conditions.[11]

Around the camp ran a wall constructed like a palisade. It was made of two-inch oak planks, with an outside walk for the sentries placed about four feet below the top of the wall. This arrangement allowed plenty of space for the sentry to fire if necessary.[12] The gates, of course, had to be reconstructed and so extended inside and out that "rushes" would be impossible. The most serious problem in camp engineering was the position of the camp latrines. It was necessary to place them at the lower edge of the camp, and below the level of the springs from which the camp got its drinking water. Because of the great number of men confined to the small area and because the soil did not drain well, it proved to be impossible to keep the ground dry.

No one had known just when the first prisoners would arrive at Camp Morton. After their capture the men were herded on river steamers and taken to St. Louis, where they were kept a few days under very bad conditions. They were then loaded on railroad cars of any kind that was available. Old passenger coaches, freight cars, and even flat cars were used, all under guard, of course. Lack of seats and any accommodations whatsoever brought the men to Indianapolis in pretty bad shape.[13]

The citizens of Indianapolis were full of forebodings at the

[10]*Official Records,* 2 series, III, 375.

[11]*Ibid.,* III, 400-1, 620-21.

[12]Indianapolis *News,* February 24, 1897, p. 6, c. 2.

[13]Indianapolis *Journal,* February 22, 1862, p. 3, c. 2; *Confederate Veteran,* V, 33 (January, 1897).

advent of a large number of prisoners. Everyone was nervous and fidgety, but very full of curiosity. The day before the prisoners came the excitement was so great that a crowd of three thousand or more persons gathered near the station to see the men brought in. No prisoners appeared,[14] but at last it was reported that an officer with his command had been ordered to meet the train the next day, February 22.[15] Then people knew something was happening.

A large crowd gathered early in the morning and waited until the middle of the afternoon, cheerfully going without dinner in the excitement. The first unit to arrive consisted of a mixed train of passenger and box cars, twenty-two in all, which, to the disappointment of the crowd, did not stop at the Union Station at all, but continued on over the tracks of the Union Railway Company to Massachusetts Avenue, where the men were detrained and marched over country roads to Camp Morton.[16]

As the train passed through the station, some of the waiting people, regardless of the orders of the guard, climbed to the roofs of the cars, riding on to the avenue with the prisoners. Women and children stood along the tracks nearly the whole distance, waving and shouting, while small boys trotted beside the train. One young man, carried away by his eagerness to see everything that was to be seen, fell in at the end of the line of prisoners and marched with them into the main gate of Camp Morton. Curiosity had got the better of his judgment. Unable to prove that he was a citizen of Indianapolis, he was held over night and forced to bunk with a "secesh" who probably felt equally outraged. The second group of prisoners was unloaded on a side track which lay across South Street about where the Pennsylvania freight station now stands and marched to the camp from there.

There is no doubt that this entry furnished the townspeople

[14]Indianapolis *Sentinel*, February 21, 1862, p. 3, c. 2.

[15]Lazarus Noble, Adjutant General's Office, Letter and Order Book No. 1, November 23, 1861-January, 1863 (Archives Division, Indiana State Library), p. 117.

[16]Indianapolis *Sentinel*, February 24, 1862, p. 2, c. 2; Indianapolis *Journal*, February 24, 1862, p. 3, c. 1, 2.

with a Roman holiday. However, the prisoners entered freely into conversation with the bystanders and goodnaturedly answered questions. The *Journal* had suggested two days before that the citizens show a kindly spirit toward the prisoners and refrain from insults to men who were powerless to resent them.[17]

The second train on Saturday brought in about four hundred prisoners; other groups came in on Sunday, Monday, and Tuesday, bringing the total number to 3,700. Some of the last to arrive were forced to spend the night in the Indianapolis and Cincinnati freight house. In the morning those at the station, 325 in all, were marched to Camp Morton; those remaining, about eight hundred, were sent on to Lafayette. About eight hundred more stopped at Terre Haute, but all of these, except a few who were too ill to be moved, were brought to Camp Morton by the middle of March. By April 1, there were five thousand men around the camp, counting both the guards and the prisoners. Squads continued to arrive during the spring and summer, often without any warning, the largest installment, over one thousand men, coming in after the battle of Shiloh.[18]

In the first groups of prisoners officers and men were commingled. Experience had already taught that it was dangerous to allow them to remain together, for the officers as a rule were prone to encourage their men to break out of camp and return South, doing what damage they could on the way. With their firm belief in the ultimate triumph of their cause, they were bound to try any plan for getting back under their own flag. In view of this fact, the officers were separated from their men and quartered in barracks on Washington Street east of the Odd Fellows Hall, which had been occupied earlier by the Nineteenth Infantry.

Most of them had lost both clothing and blankets in the confusion of their surrender. Because of their confinement

[17]February 20, 1862, p. 2, c. 1, p. 3, c. 2.

[18]Indianapolis *Sentinel,* February 24, 1862, p. 2, c. 2; February 25, p. 3, c. 2; Indianapolis *Journal,* February 24, 1862, p. 3, c. 1-2; March 10, p. 3, c. 2; Terrell, *Report,* I, 457; Noble, A. G. O., Letter and Order Book No. 1, p. 171.

food was prepared for the officers and they were permitted the privilege of buying supplementary provisions at their own expense. General Simon B. Buckner and his staff were quartered in the government building on Pennsylvania Street and their meals were brought from the Palmer House. However, the *Sentinel* of February 27, 1862, assured the public that such meals were paid for by the General out of his own pocket.[19]

One of the Turnvereins, every man of which had enlisted, rented its hall to house officers. This building stood near the northeast corner of the intersection of Meridian and Maryland streets. When officers to the number of 110 had accumulated, they were sent to Camp Chase at Columbus, Ohio, where they were kept until officers' quarters were prepared at Johnson's Island in Sandusky Harbor. General Buckner was transferred to Fort Warren.[20]

Many of the officers had with them colored servants, whose status was in doubt. They were not combatants, and they were hardly to be considered as camp followers. Halleck told Morton to let them go, if they wished to. If they chose to stay, they must be under military control.[21] Their own sentiments were summed up neatly in the announcement that "dey wasn't going to leave de boys dey came with, no how."[22] Some negroes remained at Camp Morton, and were in considerable demand as orderlies in the hospitals.

[19]Indianapolis *Journal*, February 25, 1862, p. 3, c. 1, 2; February 27, p. 3, c. 1; Indianapolis *Sentinel*, February 25, 1862, p. 3, c. 2; February 27, p. 3, c. 2. Some citizens suggested Buckner should be kept in solitary confinement. Letters of February 26, 1862, to Morton, Executive Department file, 109.9, 1861.

[20]*Official Records,* 2 series, III, 320, 333; Indianapolis *Sentinel,* February 28, 1862, p. 3, c. 1.

[21]Oliver P. Morton, Telegraphic Correspondence, February 5-June 10, 1862, pp. 56, 57, 64, 65, 66, 67 (Archives Division, Indiana State Library).

[22]Indianapolis *Sentinel,* February 24, 1862, p. 3, c. 2. An editorial in the Indianapolis *Journal,* March 29, 1862, commented bitterly because negroes who had been captured at Fort Donelson and sent to Camp Chase were still serving their masters as slaves. A report from the Assistant Inspector General of the Army to General Thomas on April 6, 1862, stated, however, that they were considered as prisoners of war, receiving exactly the same treatment as other prisoners. *Official Records,* 2 series, III, 428.

Surgeons and chaplains were allowed the freedom of the city on parole, being required to report daily at headquarters. It was at first supposed that captured physicians would exercise their vocation with their fellow prisoners. Some of these were sent to Camp Chase where they were badly needed, but after June, 1862, all were released in accordance with a general ruling that surgeons were not to be held as prisoners of war.[23]

The privates and noncommissioned officers were mostly small farmers or squatters from Mississippi, Kentucky, and Tennessee. They presented a shabby and forlorn appearance. Almost a year after the firing on Fort Sumter it was still rare to find any kind of a uniform among the prisoners. Occasionally a man would have an army blanket, either bought from England or plundered from a former United States post in the South. More common than the gray blanket was a square piece of carpet flung over the shoulders. Most of the men had a bundle of odds and ends, sometimes a bag of coffee or a slab of bacon. Few had any extra clothing, and an overcoat was unheard of.[24] Immediately numbers of them fell sick, and since the camp had no hospital facilities adequate to provide for them, they were taken to improvised hospitals in the city where overworked physicians gave them what help they could under the handicaps of poor quarters and limited equipment. The hospitals are described at greater length in Chapter IV.

The dispirited, over-fatigued men who poured into Camp Morton on February 22 and the succeeding days were nearly famished. Supplies for prisoners' camps—quarters, clothing, and rations—were normally furnished through the regular Army, but in this emergency there was no officer from the Federal Commissary Department at hand to provide for the prisoners. Commissary General Stone, of Governor Morton's staff, met the situation characteristically by ordering about four thousand rations at twenty-five cents each for prisoners

[23]Indianapolis *Sentinel*, February 25, 1862, p. 3, c. 2; Noble, A. G. O., Letter and Order Book No. 1, p. 209; *Official Records*, 2 series, IV, 45; Oliver P. Morton, Governor's Office, Letter Book, January 1, 1862 to January 17, 1863 (Archives Division, Indiana State Library), pp. 7-8.

[24]Indianapolis *Journal*, February 24, 1862, p. 3, c. 1; *Soldier of Indiana*, I, 317-18.

and guards, and securing the authorization later.[25] Blankets were also issued.[26]

The citizens offered emergency aid too, the *Sentinel* reporting on February 25 that throughout the day wagons had been progressing toward the camp in long trains, "loaded with the necessaries and comforts and even the luxuries of life." A sterner attitude was maintained by Adjutant General Lazarus Noble, who wrote to an inquirer on February 24: "Every attention will be paid to the Prisoners that their necessities and well-being demand;—anything further will not be allowed. They and their friends must reflect that they are Rebel Prisoners and as such cannot be allowed the luxuries and comforts incident to a peaceful home."[27]

In the meantime, Captain Ekin was telegraphing to his superiors for instructions about supplies for the prisoners. Like Stone, he had been driven by their necessities to act first and hope that official approval would follow. General Meigs wired to Colonel Hoffman on February 24: "Visit Chicago, Indianapolis and other places to which the prisoners taken in Tennessee have been sent. Report what is absolutely necessary to prevent their suffering. Quartermasters are in charge. Besides the rations allowed by regulations without regard to rank the United States will supply such blankets, cooking utensils and clothing as are necessary to prevent real suffering. Much clothing not good enough for troops has by fraud of inspectors and dealers been forced into our depots. This will be used. . . ." Ekin received substantially the same orders the next day.[28]

Guards for the camp had to be provided on short notice, also. As soon as Governor Morton knew that several thousand prisoners would have to be taken care of, he summoned several partially filled regiments that were being recruited in different parts of the state. The Fourteenth Battery of Light Artillery,

---

[25]*Official Records*, 2 series, III, 333. The regular cost of the ration was less than half this amount. Indianapolis *Journal*, February 25, 1862, p. 3, c. 3.

[26]*Ibid.*, p. 3, c. 2; Ekin to Morton, February 24, 1862, Executive Department file, 109.9, 1861.

[27]Noble, A. G. O., Letter and Order Book No. 1, pp. 143-44.

[28]*Official Records*, 2 series, III, 278, 316-17, 322.

under Captain Meredith H. Kidd, the Fifty-third Regiment of Indiana Volunteers, under Colonel Walter Q. Gresham, and the Sixtieth under Colonel Richard Owen all reached Indianapolis within a few days. Colonel Ben S. Nicklin, who had been commandant at Camp Morton for some months, remained in charge until these hastily summoned troops arrived, when Colonel Owen took command.[29]

Owen's appointment as commandant proved most fortunate. He was an experienced soldier. Combining strength and gentleness, he was a good disciplinarian and at the same time tempered his rulings with sympathy. From February until the middle of June, the difficult experimental months during which a workable camp routine had to be established, he handled the situation skillfully. His whole aim was to treat the prisoners in a way "calculated to make them less restless in their confinement, and likely, when they returned to their homes, to spread among their friends and acquaintances the news that they had been deceived regarding northern men."[30]

At this period no general rules for the supervision of prisoners had been laid down. While Colonel Hoffman pleaded that such matters be delegated exclusively to his department, the generals in the field continued to exercise a good deal of authority over the movements of prisoners, and each camp commandant set up his own disciplinary measures. A few very general instructions regarding prisoners held in Indiana were issued by Adjutant General Noble under order of Governor Morton on February 24.[31] Prisoners were to be

[29]Noble, A. G. O., Letter and Order Book No. 1, pp. 114, 118, 130; Indianapolis *Journal,* February 24, 1862, p. 3, c. 1-2; February 28, p. 3, c. 1; Indianapolis *Sentinel,* February 24, 1862, p. 3, c. 2. Gresham's regiment, with which the Sixty-second was consolidated, was ordered to join Halleck on March 14, and Kidd's Battery followed on April 10. Noble, *op. cit.,* pp. 169, 170, 190, 194, 197. A battalion of the Sixty-third Regiment, under Lieutenant Colonel John S. Williams, and some companies from the Sixty-first Regiment, under Colonel Bernard F. Mullen, which had been guarding prisoners at Lafayette and Terre Haute respectively, took their places as guards at Camp Morton, remaining until late in May, 1862. Terrell, *Report,* II, 587, 595.

[30]Indianapolis *Journal,* April 17, 1862, p. 2, c. 1; April 21, p. 2, c. 1-2.

[31]Noble, A. G. O., Letter and Order Book No. 1, p. 131.

COLONEL RICHARD OWEN
COMMANDANT
CAMP MORTON PRISON 1862
TRIBVTE BY CONFEDERATE PRISONERS
OF WAR AND THEIR FRIENDS
FOR HIS COVRTESY AND KINDNESS
★ ★ ★ ★ ★ ★ ★ ★ ★ ★

thrown into their original company organizations, each company in charge of its highest noncommissioned officer, and were to be subsisted in that order, receiving the same rations, clothing, and equipment as Indiana troops. No communication with citizens was to be allowed. Finally, company rolls were to be prepared. Beyond this, Owen had to formulate his own rules. He drew up a humane and sensible code, much of which was later incorporated into Hoffman's instructions to all commandants of prisoners' camps.[32]

"Rules for Camp Morton.

"1. The entire camp prisoners will be divided into thirty divisions, each under charge of a chief selected by the companies composing the division from among the first sergeants of companies. At the bugle call for first sergeants they will report themselves at headquarters.

"2. These chiefs of divisions will draw up the provision returns for their divisions, care for and be responsible for the general appearance, police and welfare of their divisions. The first fifteen will constitute a board of appeal for the hearing of grievances, settlement and punishment of misdemeanors, subject to the approval of the commander of the post in their fifteen divisions. The other fifteen will form a like court for the remaining fifteen divisions.

"3. Among the crimes and misdemeanors against which first sergeants are expected to guard and which they will punish on detection are counterfeiting the commandant's, doctor's, adjutant's or chaplain's hands for requisitions, making improper use of premises, refusing to take a reasonable share in the details according to the roster, selling to the sutler any articles issued to them as clothing, appropriating things belonging to others or insulting sentinels.

"4. The prisoners' returns will be handed in for approval at 10 a. m. each alternate day previous to the one on which the issue is made. The issues of tobacco and stationery will be made on Wednesdays and Saturdays at 2 p. m. by the chaplains, as well as the distribution of reading matter. Letters will be

[32]*Official Records,* 2 series, III, 518-19.

given out between 2 and 3 p. m. and mailed between 3 and 4 p. m.

"5. Daily inspections will be made by the commandant or officer of the day to see that the policing so essential to health has been thoroughly performed, and facilities will be afforded for sports and athletic exercise also conducive to health, as well as bathing by companies, if permission can be obtained from the proper authority.

"6. The first sergeants of companies will look after the general wants of their companies and maintain the necessary order, discipline and police essential to health and comfort, and will make requisitions, first on chiefs of divisions, and they afterwards at headquarters, for clothing, camp and garrison equipage absolutely necessary; also for tobacco wanted, and the like.

"7. The inside chain of soldiers, except a small patrol with side-arms, will be removed, and the quiet and good order of the camp as well as the policing for health and comfort, the construction of new sinks when necessary and the daily throwing in of lime and mold to prevent bad odors will be entirely under the supervision of the sergeants of prisoners.

"8. Vessels for the washing of clothing and ropes for clothes lines will be furnished, and no bed or other clothing will be put on roof tops or on fences.

"9. Prisoners will carefully avoid interrupting sentinels in the discharge of their duty, and especially will not curse them, use abusive language or climb onto fences or trees, as the sentinels are ordered to fire if such an offense occurs after three positive and distinct orders to desist, even in day time. At night only one warning will be given to any one climbing on the fence tops.

"10. A prisoners' fund will be created by the deduction as heretofore of small amounts from the rations of beef, bread, beans, &c., a schedule of which will be placed at the commissary department. This fund will be used for the purchase of tobacco, stationery, stamps and such other articles as the chiefs of divisions may report, and which should be drawn on requisitions handed in by first sergeants between 9 and 10 a. m. each day.

"11. Every endeavor will be made by the commandant to give each and every prisoner as much liberty and comfort as is consistent with orders received and with an equal distribution of the means at disposal, provided such indulgence never leads to any abuse of the privileges."

These rules established virtual self-government among the prisoners. They worked well, with occasional exceptions that necessitated modifications and curtailments of privileges. Sometimes the townspeople were inclined to criticize their latitude, but they earned for Owen the undying gratitude of many prisoners.

Company rolls remained a problem throughout the war. If no muster roll came with the prisoners, new ones had to be made immediately. They were called every morning.[33] Some of them were written on sheets of legal cap, pasted together in long strips, and ruled off by hand into columns for name, company, enlistment, time and place of joining, capture, transfer, or death. The beginning of the roll might be handsomely engrossed, but the handwriting was often illegible. Prisoners who had crimes on their consciences and preferred not to be traced sometimes gave false names. A spirit of mischief induced others to offer ridiculous names, which got them into trouble when exchange rolls were prepared. The chief difficulty, of course, was due to transfers to hospitals and to deaths among the prisoners.

Besides keeping the rolls for the camps the commandants were requested toward the end of April, 1862, to send a complete list to the Commissary General of Prisoners and monthly reports thereafter. In spite of the fact that the rolls were checked each morning, and that requisitions for rations were also supposed to be checked against them, Owen reported that

[33]The Indianapolis *Sentinel* of February 28, 1862, p. 3, c. 3, announced that rolls of all the prisoners had been made out and were in Owen's hands. The morning roll call was handled as follows. Owen called the roll for one of the thirty divisions of prisoners; the chaplain, the ten first lieutenants and the ten second lieutenants of his regiment each called one roll, taking care of twenty-two divisions; the rolls for the remaining divisions were called by officers from assisting guard regiments. Owen to Morton, April 20, 1862, Sixtieth Regiment Indiana Volunteers file, folder C, Archives Division, Indiana State Library.

he had, found enough discrepancies to necessitate a thorough revision.[34] No one ever did manage to have the rolls complete and exact.

During the first rather disorganized months the noncommissioned Confederate officers in charge of companies were almost as busy as the commandant. Besides requisitioning the proper amount of rations, they had to divide them out fairly among the men. The slightest partiality provoked a storm of no mean proportions. There was inevitably one, or more, in each group who stole from his comrades. Cooks had to stand guard over provisions, and honest and hungry men formed the habit of eating the whole day's ration as soon as it was received, or of carrying it in their haversacks for safekeeping.[35] Anyone caught at petty thieving or similar misdemeanors was punished by the prisoners themselves.

Criticism about rations had been bad enough when Indiana recruits were trained at Camp Morton. Now they were much worse. For example, the Southerners were accustomed to lean bacon, and they complained at being supplied with bacon that was fat, or at best had a streak of fat and a streak of lean. They declared that the beef was all bone and the bread all sour. For the time being, baker's bread of good quality was served, for it was the cheapest way to provide bread for the prisoners, but these southern boys wanted "good cawn pone, with drippin's." The *Sentinel* suggested that the commissary department buy meal in the open market and furnish

[34]*Official Records,* 2 series, III, 502, 515; IV, 152; Indianapolis *Sentinel,* February 24, 1862, p. 3, c. 2. The *Sentinel* of March 17 (p. 1, c. 2-6), lists the prisoners confined at Camp Morton, giving a total of 3,233. The issue of March 18 (p. 3, c. 1) lists 278 prisoners at Terre Haute who were still to be transferred to Camp Morton.

[35][S. A. Cunningham], *Memorials: Col. Richard Owen, the Good Samaritan of Camp Morton . . .* (Nashville, Tenn., n. d.), p. 4. Quarrels over the division of rations sometimes resulted in the death of a prisoner. On one occasion a sergeant in charge of a division of prisoners was accused of dividing rations unfairly. The sergeant punched his accuser with a stick of firewood, whereupon the enraged man seized a club and knocked the sergeant down, clubbing him so that he died in about six hours. Indianapolis *Journal,* May 19, 1862, p. 3, c. 1; May 21, p. 3, c. 2; Indianapolis *Sentinel,* May 19, 1862, p. 3, c. 1; May 22, p. 3, c. 2. See also *Confederate Veteran,* XVI, xxxvi (December, 1908).

it to the men, but it was impossible to allow each boy to cook his pone "the way it orter be."[36]

After Colonel Hoffman visited the camp early in March, he proposed the erection of a camp bakehouse, a practical suggestion that effected a large saving to the Government. The great cost of prisoners' camps was a serious problem. The sums involved seem small to us, but the citizen of 1862 was more appalled by a national debt of one billion dollars than we are by forty billion. The contractor for the camp was obliged to buy a full army ration for every prisoner. A pound of flour thus supplied would make almost a pound and a third of good bread, and with the baking done in a camp bakehouse, the profit would go to the camp and not to the baker.

Hoffman's suggestion was approved and he immediately wrote to Captain Ekin for estimates on the cost of a bakehouse large enough to bake for five thousand men. It was to consist of a single large room with a floor, a shingle roof, and walls of upright boarding battened. Later in the month he directed that the commissary at the camp withhold any part of the prisoners' rations which might be in excess of their needs, and semimonthly pay to Colonel Owen the value of the ration so retained. The fund thus accumulated was to be used to purchase "brooms, buckets, table furniture" and other articles for the prisoners, which would otherwise be an additional expense to the Government. The bakehouse went into operation about the middle of April, and Ekin later reported that the ovens were working well and that a fund of $2,400 had been accumulated by May 1.[37]

Out of the fund were bought "tobacco, stationery, stamps, wheel barrows and tools for policing, scissors for cutting the hair, plank and nails for making bunks, lines for airing clothes,

[36]Indianapolis *Journal*, March 11, 1862, p. 3, c. 2; Indianapolis *Sentinel*, February 28, 1862, p. 3, c. 1. The newspapers were not above poking fun at this passionate attachment to corn pone. The *Sentinel* of March 8 (p. 2, c. 4), quoted the suggestion of the Lafayette *Journal* that there was an "inscrutable reason for compelling these maize-loving rebels to eat Northern wheat bread," and that "with every mouthful . . . the hungry rebel swallows and incorporates in his treasonable system so much loyalty and patriotism."

[37]*Official Records*, 2 series, III, 349, 375, 386-87, 401, 432, 562; Indianapolis *Journal*, March 22, 1862, p. 3, c. 1; Terrell, *Report*, I, 449.

leather for mending shoes, thread for repairs, &c.; also additional vegetables, such as potatoes and onions, and some extra supplies of molasses."[38]

Hoffman had delegated control of the fund to Owen, with instructions that strict account of expenditures be kept, with the bills. Owen was doubtless too occupied with other business of the camp to handle it himself, for Ekin wrote to Hoffman on May 21 that a council of administration had been instituted at Camp Morton, and had taken charge of the disbursements. Ekin was excluded from this council. He was dissatisfied with the arrangement, and asked that control of the fund be placed in his hands, on the ground that various expenditures which should be paid from it would not be made unless under his direction. He promised he would always confer with Owen and the post quartermaster, Lieutenant J. J. Palmer.[39] It is likely that Hoffman and Ekin expected to take care of more ambitious expenditures than those heretofore made from the fund, and as Ekin's suggestion was later carried out, the rapidly increasing sums were used to supplement the hospital fund, for the erection of additional buildings, payment of civilian employees, and the like.

To return to the chiefs of divisions: having served out the food to the best of his ability, the sergeant in charge was obliged to see that the clean straw supplied for the bunks was equally apportioned. If left unguarded it had a way of disappearing. Quantities of straw about the camp presented a fire hazard that demanded unceasing vigilance; smoking was restricted, for in a high wind a fire would have produced a major tragedy. Company chiefs also had to detail men to police the camp, and to act as hospital orderlies and as grave diggers.

Reports about needed clothing also went through the sergeant's hands. Prisoners were allowed to receive supplies from home, but the garments sent were sometimes impractical. The girl who sent her imprisoned boy friend a pair of embroidered slippers, for example, was not likely to keep his

[38]Owen to Editor, Indianapolis *Journal,* April 18, 1862, in *Official Records,* 2 series, III, 516. See also Owen's Rule 10, *ante,* p. 264.

[39]*Official Records,* 2 series, III, 562-63.

devotion. A pair of thick warm socks and a sweater would have been welcome enough, but good saxony yarn was an unknown quantity in the blockaded South, and such gifts were out of the question.[40]

The intention of the Federal Government to issue clothing and blankets when needed is clear, but in practice these good intentions were only partially fulfilled. Prisoners received clothing which had been furnished to the United States by contractors and condemned by government inspectors. It sometimes happened that the condemned articles were not those most needed in the prison camps, or that shipments were delayed—transportation constituted a big expense and shipments to troops in the field were given preference.[41]

At Camp Morton, though blankets were issued to the prisoners who had none,[42] a sudden drop in temperature caused extreme suffering among men unaccustomed to a northern climate. The Ladies Patriotic Societies and the Sanitary Commission responded generously to calls for assistance, and during 1862 the prisoners made few complaints of poor treatment.

Would-be visitors made their appearance before the prisoners were fairly settled. Governor Morton ruled immediately that there was to be no communication between citizens or guards and camp inmates, and Owen enforced the rule. A notice of the regulation was sent to the Louisville *Journal* on February 26; nevertheless many Kentuckians made the long hard trip to Indianapolis in the hope of seeing their relatives or friends. Neither masculine indignation nor feminine wiles succeeded in getting them into camp. This rule, harsh as it must have seemed in many cases, tended to prevent unrest among the prisoners, and Captain Ekin commended it highly to Secretary of War Stanton. Adjutant General Noble at the

[40]For the effect of the blockade on the South, see J. B. Jones, *A Rebel War Clerk's Diary at the Confederate States Capital* (2 volumes. Philadelphia, J. B. Lippincott & Co., 1866).

[41]*Official Records,* 2 series, III, 316-17, 335-36. It should be remembered that the Federal Government had no intention of supplying clothes that would be convertible into Confederate uniforms, should prisoners be exchanged.

[42]Ekin to Governor Morton, February 24, 1862, Executive Department file, 109.9, 1861.

same time protested against the laxity at Camp Chase, where "avowedly disloyal" visitors were admitted. The result was a tightening of restrictions in other camps, and commendation of the discipline at Camp Morton.[43]

Communication by mail was not cut off. Prisoners could write home—the newspapers asked for donations of stamps for the prisoners' mail—and letters, money, clothing, and other donations were allowed to enter the camp after proper inspection. Assistant Adjutant General James Wilson handled this for a time,[44] but by the middle of March, 1862, censorship and inspection duties were taking the entire time of two important officers, and Colonel Owen appealed to Governor Morton for someone who could take charge of the post office and inspect presents for the prisoners.[45] Abel Evans was thereupon appointed special postmaster for Camp Morton to take charge of all mail. After carefully inspecting the letters written, Evans endorsed each envelope "prisoner's letter," "inspected," signed it, mailed all that were within the Union lines and returned the rest to the Adjutant General's office to be forwarded under a flag of truce. Likewise, he took charge of all letters for prisoners arriving by mail or otherwise, and inspected them before delivering them.[46]

Letters were given out between two and three o'clock in the afternoon and could be mailed out between three and four.[47] To reduce the great labor of inspection an order was issued at this time that prisoners might write only to relatives and immediate friends. Evidently the request was not obeyed, for nearly a month later, Adjutant General Noble sent Colonel Owen a number of copies of the order to distribute "freely" among the prisoners. He said that he, himself, had burned a number of letters from four to eight pages long, and that half

[43]Noble, A. G. O., Letter and Order Book No. 1, p. 131; Indianapolis *Journal*, February 25, 1862, p. 3, c. 2; March 17, p. 3, c. 1; *Official Records*, 2 series, III, 411, 412.

[44]Indianapolis *Journal*, February 27, 1862, p. 3, c. 2; March 17, p. 3, c. 2.

[45]Richard Owen file, March 13, 1862, Archives Division, Indiana State Library.

[46]Noble, A. G. O., Letter and Order Book No. 1, p. 172. See also *Confederate Veteran*, II, 115 (April, 1894), VI, 583 (January, 1898).

[47]*Ante*, pp. 263-64.

of them or more, were to mere acquaintances and of little importance. Evans was expected to reject and destroy this kind. A Federal order issued later in the summer and sent to all camps, limited letters to one page only, the contents to be of a strictly private nature.[48]

The censor's task was not always dull. The following lines from a southern girl to "Dear John" at Camp Morton were published in the Indianapolis *Journal* and copied in papers throughout the country:[49] "I will be for Jeffdavise til the tenisee river freazes over, and then be for him, and scrach on the ice

"Jeffdavise rides a white horse,
Lincoln rides a mule,
Jeffdavise is a gentleman,
Lincoln is a fule.

"I wish I could send them lincon devels some pies, they would never want any more to eat in this world."

All material contributed to the camp locally, such as newspapers and books, had to be examined for fear that weapons or tools might be concealed between the leaves. Packages sent to the prisoners from home were carefully examined by the censor and contraband materials taken out. Jellies and other delicacies were confiscated for hospital use.[50]

For a time, money which the prisoners brought with them, or which they received while at camp, seems to have been entirely at their disposal.[51] But because attempts at bribery were suspected, or because officials thought too much money was going into the hands of the camp sutler, General Noble decreed on May 2, 1862, that no money should be delivered to prisoners except through the commandant's hands, that no prisoners receive more than a dollar or two a week for necessaries, and that any funds remaining to a prisoner's credit

[48]Indianapolis *Journal,* March 19, 1862, p. 3, c. 3; Noble, A. G. O., Letter and Order Book No. 1, pp. 172, 205; *Official Records, 2* series, IV, 153.

[49]Indianapolis *Journal,* May 6, 1862, p. 3, c. 2.

[50]*Indiana Soldier,* I, 319.

[51]The Indianapolis *Journal,* April 8, 1862, p. 3, c. 4, mentions "about $6,000 received lately, and distributed among the rebel prisoners at Camp Morton." The *Journal* surmised that most of this money, sent by relatives in Kentucky and Tennessee, went into the sutlers' pockets.

should be held by the commandant, to be doled out in small quantities.[52]

Unauthorized sutlers thronged to every training camp and prison. They had to be watched continually to prevent sale of contraband, and to protect the prisoners from being overcharged. At some camps they became very wealthy, but regulatory precautions were taken early at Camp Morton. There were doubtless some unauthorized venders of goods about, and the regimental sutlers attached to the Sixtieth and Fifty-third Regiments probably supplied the camp to some extent, but shortly after the arrival of the first prisoners, Governor Morton appointed a post sutler, Nathan Crawford. Prisoners' purchases of small articles were supposed thereafter to be made through him. Much friction attended the attempt to prevent sutlers from competing, and nothing but threat of arrest was effective in keeping them away from camp.[53]

Owen evidently considered literary works outside the sutlers' line. At any rate he allowed William Gibson and a "Mr. Keatting" to sell books and periodicals in the camp, defending the procedure as "beneficial to the Prisoners by keeping them occupied & contented." He also secured several hundred books for them from the superintendent of public instruction.[54]

When free men constantly chafe against restrictions, how much more likely that prisoners of war, humiliated by their capture and depressed by hardships and illness should fret against camp discipline. In spite of their labors at policing, "KP" duty, and at the hospitals and cemeteries, the prisoners had many empty hours which Owen gave them every latitude in filling with such amusements as they could devise.

Fraternal organizations such as the Masons and Odd Fellows, sent a friendly greeting to prisoner members, and groups from these orders were allowed to meet at the camp in what had once been the headquarters of the Board of

[52]Noble, A. G. O., Letter and Order Book No. 1, p. 225.
[53]*Ibid.*, pp. 157, 553, 556.
[54]Memorandum, April 26, 1862, Richard Owen file, Archives Division, Indiana State Library; Indianapolis *Sentinel,* April 11, 1862, p. 3, c. 1.

Agriculture.[55] Prisoners with anxious mothers or sweethearts could have their pictures taken at Mr. Charles D. Vajen's "Daguerrian or Photographic establishment." This was authorized in March. Vajen was allowed to employ only two assistants, the three of them being commanded to have no intercourse with the prisoners beyond what was demanded by their business, and to carry no letters or messages.[56] The stream of daguerreotypes that flowed from Camp Morton to Kentucky, Tennessee, and Mississippi must have carried comfort to the folks at home, no matter how blurry the print or how stary-eyed the subject.

Music was another palliative. Though camp regulations discouraged the prisoners from congregating in groups of more than two or three, especially at night, they were allowed to form more than one glee club, and a band of Ethiopian minstrels gave concerts now and then. On one occasion the prisoners serenaded the officers with "Dixie" and a collection of other secession songs. A few weeks later, the band of the United States Regulars gave a concert at the camp. We have no record of their program, but it must have been chosen with extreme care, for according to the *Sentinel* it "enlivened the hearts of both prisoners and citizens."[57] Besides the singers there were some fair actors in the camp, who were allowed to arrange dramatic entertainments for the hospitals. One is said to have taken the oath of allegiance, become a member of the old Metropolitan Company, and remained in Indianapolis for years after the war.[58]

In the big central area of the camp ball games were permitted. Another great resource of the prisoner was whittling. Thousands of handmade souvenirs still exist: pipe bowls of many materials, brooches cut from beef bones, and puzzles of the common sort were made in quantity; rings whittled

[55]*Ibid.,* February 24, 1862, p. 3, c. 2; Indianapolis *Journal,* July 28, 1862, p. 3, c. 1.

[56]Noble, A. G. O., Letter and Order Book No. 1, p. 173.

[57]Indianapolis *Sentinel,* March 26, 1862, p. 3, c. 1; May 13, p. 3, c. 1; Indianapolis *Journal,* July 28, p. 3, c. 1.

[58]Indianapolis *News,* February 24, 1897, p. 6, c. 2.

from rubber buttons and inlaid with silver stars cut from dimes were fashionable; others were carved out of cannel coal.[59]

Unfortunately a brisk contraband trade in these articles developed through the newsboys who entered the camp. Worse still was the fact that the prisoners had been allowed to keep the knives with which they whittled, and even old pistols of the heirloom variety. This gave rise in May to rumors that a great number of "arms" had been smuggled to the prisoners. Regretfully Owen ordered these sorry weapons turned in. They were delivered promptly—some forty or fifty "antique, half-cocked and empty pistols" and about three times as many knives. Each article, carefully labeled with its owner's name, was put away to be redelivered when the prisoners were exchanged or liberated. The *Sentinel* commented tartly: "it indicates a singular want of confidence, on the part of any portion of the community, in Col. Owen, who has proved himself a most able and vigilant officer, to intimate that his vigilance could permit arms to be smuggled into Camp Morton."[60]

There had been some criticism of Owen's leniency before this date. It had been his practice to allow prisoners to visit their comrades in the hospital. The privilege was extended "to permit some of the sergeants of Prisoners to make a few purchases under the charge of officers who pledged themselves that there should be no interviews."[61] On April 15 a little group started for the business district. They made purchases here and there, then, unluckily for themselves, their fellow prisoners, and Owen, part of them stopped at a saloon and "imbibed freely." Worse still, they bootlegged liquor back to camp, and by night some of the prisoners were so exhilarated that they threw stones and beef bones at the sergeant of the guard. One of the guards was sent posthaste for Owen, but before he could return a well-aimed beef bone knocked the sergeant off his feet. Without waiting for Owen's counsel,

[59]"Treatment of Prisoners at Camp Morton," *Century Magazine*, XLII, 770 (September, 1891).

[60]Indianapolis *Sentinel*, May 31, 1862, p. 3, c. 2.

[61]Owen to Morton, April 16, 1862, in Sixtieth Regiment Indiana Volunteers file, folder C.

he ordered his men to fire. Four men were injured, two slightly, and two so seriously that they had to be sent to the hospital next day. The battery of artillery which commanded the camp, alarmed by the firing within the wall, hastily fired a round of blank cartridges. Presumably this and Owen's appearance settled the camp for the night, but the episode was not closed. Governor Morton called for an explanation, and both *Sentinel* and *Journal* wanted to know how such a situation could arise.[62]

Owen wrote to the Governor on April 16. He told under what instructions the expedition had been allowed and announced the suspension of similar privileges in future. He had not been able to discover which men threw rocks at the guard, but said that the prisoners had "promised to bring them to speedy punishment (saying that hanging was too good for them)." He intimated that if the Governor disapproved of the system adopted or knew of someone who could carry out his views better, "the officers & Soldiers of the Sixtieth would feel grateful for the change." He called attention to the high mortality among his overworked men, and mentioned that he had been informed there was no prospect of his receiving any pay for the past six months' services.[63]

Two days later he wrote to the *Journal* at greater length, setting forth his aims, the general system of the camp, and the unending demands on himself and his men. "I have never spent one night from camp since I was ordered here," he wrote, "nor entered a hotel or saloon since my arrival. After a heavy day's work, I sometimes, at night, retire to my camp cot, without divesting myself of either coat or boots, in order to be ready at the slightest noise for my responsible and onerous duties." He called attention with justifiable pride to the small number of escapes from the camp proper, only 13 out of 4,200 prisoners, part of whom had been recaptured and brought back.[64]

[62]Indianapolis *Journal*, April 17, 1862, p. 2, c. 1; Indianapolis *Sentinel*, April 17, 1862, p. 3, c. 2; Noble, A. G. O., Letter and Order Book No. 1, p. 204.

[63]Sixtieth Regiment Indiana Volunteers file, folder C.

[64]Indianapolis *Journal*, April 21, 1862, p. 2, c. 1-2.

Another well-intentioned concession to the prisoners resulted in much the same way. As the days grew warmer, squads of prisoners were taken daily to Fall Creek, under guard, for bathing. On a day in June a party of five or six inveigled their guards into allowing an examination of their new Enfield rifles. The guards were overpowered in a flash, and the prisoners proceeded southward.[65]

Prisoners acting as hospital orderlies sometimes succeeded in slipping away, as the hospital guards were few. It was not so easy to get away from Camp Morton. Captain Kidd's Battery of Light Artillery deserved part of the credit for this. As a reassurance to the citizens or a warning to the prisoners—perhaps both—the *Sentinel* announced immediately after the arrival of the first Confederates that the battery was stationed "about Camp Morton, commanding every entrance and exit and all the buildings and every acre for miles around."[66] There were sentries on the wall and, for a time at least, a chain of guards stationed inside it. These were later reduced to small patrols with side arms. Sentinels were ordered to fire at any prisoner who persisted in ignoring three "positive and distinct" orders to desist from a violation of rules, such as climbing on the fence. At night only one order was required.[67]

Toward the end of March, a prisoner was wounded while attempting to pass the guard. A few days later Governor Morton appointed a special officer to arrest and bring back escaped prisoners; and the same day word went to the camp that all recaptured prisoners would be sent to the Marion County jail for close confinement in irons.[68] The jail was not popular. Six prisoners inhabiting that *"low and degraded Den"* asked for a minister of the gospel to sing and pray with them. One of the signers was a George McCormick, whose mess mates later petitioned that he might be allowed to return

---

[65]Indianapolis *Sentinel,* May 16, 1862, p. 3, c. 2; June 14, p. 3, c. 1; Madison *Courier* (daily), June 16, 1862, p. 2, c. 1.

[66]Indianapolis *Sentinel,* February 24, 1862, p. 3, c. 2.

[67]Rule 9, *ante,* p. 264.

[68]Indianapolis *Journal,* April 1, 1862, p. 3, c. 3; Noble, A. G. O., Letter and Order Book No. 1, pp. 195, 196.

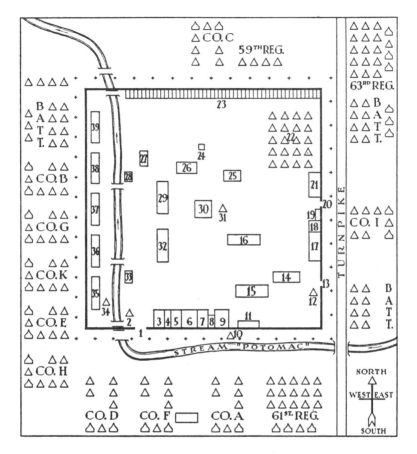

CAMP MORTON, 1862, adapted from map by E. S. Thrall, Sixtieth Regiment Indiana Volunteers. 1. Entrance. 2. Officer of gate. 3. Drummers. 4. Barber. 5. Picture gallery. 6. Majors. 7. Chaplain. 8. Steward. 9. Colonel. 10. Magazine. 11. Stable. 12. Wagon master. 13. Gate. 14-16. Barracks. 17. Commissary, 60th Regiment. 18. Bakery. 19. Stable. 20. Gate. 21. Commissary, 63d Regiment. 22-23. Prisoners' tents, shed. 24. Preacher's stand (Parson Brownlow). 25. Surgeon. 26. Sutler. 27. Picture car. 28. Post office. 29. Barracks. 30. Doctor. 31. Hospital tent. 32. Receiving hospital. 33. Dispensary. 34. Prisoners' tent. 35-39. Barracks 1-5. + Sentinels. Guard companies, unless otherwise indicated, belonged to the 60th Regiment. Batteries were Captain Coulson's, Captain Nicklin's, and Captain Von Schlen's.

to camp, to share their "comparatively light imprisonment."[69]

About this time the guards were issued revolvers in addition to the usual arms, to be used in case of attempted prison breaks. Kidd's Battery was withdrawn in the middle of April, and this fact may have stimulated in the prisoners new hopes of escape. Following rumors of an intended stampede, the sentinels were doubled, and the patrols inside the camp increased.[70]

Accidents happened, with the camp full of unrest and the guards tense and nervous. One Sunday night about nine o'clock, one of the prisoners mounted a rise in the grounds from which he could see over the wall. He was hailed by the sentry and ordered to move. But the guard was being changed, and in the clatter of orders, the prisoner, as he explained later, did not hear the sentinel's challenge. He did not move, and the sentry fired, wounding him slightly. The man was a Baptist preacher. His statement that he had no intention of disobeying an order was believed, and he escaped the further misery of being dragged off to jail. In spite of the tightened discipline, a prisoner occasionally escaped, or was wounded in the attempt.[71]

One nineteen-year-old youth tried to escape in women's clothes. Said the *Sentinel,* directing its sarcasm impartially at guards and prisoner: "He was not shot at, for a wonder, but came down to the valiant sentinel voluntarily. He cut an excellent figure the next morning as he was led to jail personating a beautiful and blushing secession damsel."[72]

Camp discipline was badly strained on one occasion when Governor Morton brought a visitor to address the men. The

[69]Petitions of April 25 and May 28, 1862, to Governor Morton, Executive Department file, 109.9, 1861, Archives Division, Indiana State Library. By June 3, there were eighteen recaptured prisoners in the jail. Indianapolis *Journal,* June 3, 1862, p. 3, c. 1. See also the *Sentinel,* May 21, 1862, p. 3, c. 2.

[70]Noble, A. G. O., Letter and Order Book No. 1, pp. 198, 212.

[71]Indianapolis *Journal,* April 30, 1862, p. 3, c. 2; May 6, p. 3, c. 3; June 2, p. 3, c. 1; Indianapolis *Sentinel,* April 11, 1862, p. 3, c. 1; May 6, p. 3, c. 1; *Confederate Veteran,* V, 15 (January, 1897); VI, 537 (November, 1898); XXXV, 456-60 (December, 1927).

[72]Indianapolis *Sentinel,* June 7, 1862, p. 3, c. 1.

Reverend William G. Brownlow, a violently Unionist minister and newspaper editor of Knoxville, Tennessee, was thoroughly detested by the Confederates. To dispose of him, they sent him within the Union lines in the spring of 1862. He began a series of lectures in the northern states, reaching Indianapolis in April. A speech from Parson Brownlow was more than the "obstreperous and unrepentant" Kentuckians could bear. They jeered and shouted, called him "the old traitor," and begged to have him put out.[73]

A constant grievance with the prisoners was the epithet "rebel." When the *Journal* capped this by referring to some of them as "rowdy rebels," they promptly invited the editor to visit the camp, promising a "*cord*-ial reception."[74]

Even when the prisoners were not trying to escape or booing distinguished visitors, they could make a guard's life miserable. Keeping always on the alert, watching and listening, wearied the nerves. It amused the prisoners to start rumors—analogous to the ghost stories of civilian life—filled with references to plans for escape. Or they would entertain themselves by mimicking the cries of men in pain or delirium. Their success in annoying the sentries accounts for the story, probably apocryphal, that a home guard, on the night of an eclipse, fired at his own shadow, mistaking it for a rebel prisoner.[75]

During the first weeks, the guards ploughed their beats in mud "shoe-mouth" deep. As a preventive to sickness, the Adjutant General arranged for the laying of walks, and asked for some Sibley tents with floors and stoves.[76] A house for the guards on duty was later built outside the wall, and paid for from the prisoners' fund.[77] Their regular quarters lay

[73]*Confederate Veteran*, XVIII, 334 (July, 1910) ; Indianapolis *Journal*, April 9, 1862, p. 3, c. 1.

[74]*Ibid.*, April 29, 1862, p. 3, c. 2.

[75]*Ibid.*, June 14, 1862, p. 3, c. 1.

[76]Noble, A. G. O., Letter and Order Book No. 1, pp. 148, 149-50; Indianapolis *Journal*, March 9, 1862, p. 3, c. 2. A Sibley tent when pitched was about twelve feet high, conical, and would accommodate twenty men for sleeping purposes. *Annals of the Fifty-Seventh Regiment Indiana Volunteers . . .* (Dayton, Ohio, 1868), p. 20.

[77]*Official Records*, 2 series, III, 621.

south of Camp Morton between Nineteenth and Tinker (now Sixteenth) streets, and came to be known as Camp Burnside.[78] Owen's force was not large in proportion to the number of men to be guarded. His regiment was not at full strength when he was summoned to Indianapolis in February, and he continued recruiting in addition to all his duties as commandant at Camp Morton. None of the organizations which assisted the Sixtieth—the Fifty-third, and Kidd's Battery of Light Artillery, succeeded by a battalion from the Sixty-third Regiment and some companies from the Sixty-first—remained at the camp for any length of time. On May 4, 1862, Owen called Colonel Hoffman's attention to the fact that he was guarding over four thousand men with a minimum regiment and 207 men from another, while at Camp Chase there were two regiments to guard about a thousand prisoners.[79] The men were overworked, and the death rate among them was as high as among the regiments in the field.[80]

One of Owen's duties was the examination of petitions on behalf of the prisoners.[81] Their variety was astonishing, though most of them had the same basic purpose, to secure a release or parole. Unionist fathers from Kentucky and Tennessee asked the release of their sons, offering security for their conduct during the remainder of the war. The commander of a force of Federal soldiers which had captured a group of young Confederates from the same county, wrote that the prisoners were truly repentant and requested their parole. An Indianan told how his brother had been persuaded to leave home, how he had gone to Arkansas, started homeward, and on the way had been impressed into the Confederate Army at Memphis.

Some petitioners were modest in their requests: for example, a Kentuckian asked only that his nephew be transferred

[78]"Oldfish on Memorials," in Indianapolis *News*, August 15, 1913, p. 6, c. 5.

[79]*Official Records*, 2 series, III, 515.

[80]Owen to Morton, April 16, 1862, Sixtieth Regiment Indiana Volunteers file, folder C; Report from City Hospital, Indianapolis *Journal*, April 29, 1862, p. 3, c. 3; *Official Records*, 2 series, III, 515.

[81]There are three folders of these petitions in the Archives Division, Indiana State Library, Executive Department file, 109.9, 1861.

from prison quarters at St. Louis to join his comrades at Camp Morton. At the other extreme was the gentleman who confided to Governor Morton that he wanted his son released, but hoped to have him stay in school at Indianapolis for two years; he asked that the Governor would help him find a good boarding place. Occasionally people wrote protesting against a release or calling attention to some prisoner who had deserted the Union forces to join the South.

Petitions from the prisoners show an equal variety. Requests for full or limited parole often followed some family catastrophe, children left helpless, a sick sister, a dying wife or mother. Wounds and ailments induced others to apply for parole or discharge, and physicians and comrades frequently joined forces to help these cases. We have no record of the action taken on the majority of these appeals. In one case, Adjutant General Noble instructed Owen to release a boy who had been impressed into service, and since the Government made no arrangement for transportation in such instances, he suggested turning the boy loose, with a note recommending him to the charity of railroad and steamboat lines.[82]

Among the more unusual petitions is one from a Scot who had lost his job in the South and entered the army in desperation. He asked to be released to return to Scotland. A German, also, in platelike script begged to be freed to return to the Fatherland. One curious case involved a free colored man and his nephew who had been arrested for aiding the rebels. Some of the petitioners were willing to use any means to help themselves. One man asked Owen if he could not be got off "without exciting any suspicion," and four members of a fraternal organization to which he belonged, promised never to tell if Owen could manage their discharge.

Some of the petitions show how successfully Owen had preached his doctrine that the Union was worth preserving. A private from Tennessee wrote to Morton: "I thought that I was fighting enimies but I am sadly mistaken." Numbers of Tennesseans asserted that they had been forced into service. "I was always a union man and am one til yet," wrote one of

[82]Letter of March 19, 1862, Noble, A. G. O., Letter and Order Book No. I, p. 174.

this group to Owen. "I voted against the stait going out all the time I had nothinge to Doo with the rebelyan from the first to the last and when Harris made his last cal for thirty thousand troups theay Drafted me in the sirvise. . . . I want your advice what to do." Fear of the three-year draft induced numbers of Union sympathizers who could not go North to enlist for one year as volunteers. The idea of abolition was still abhorrent to most of the prisoners, however, and one man spoke for many of his comrades when he said: "I am a union man that is to say I am not an abolitionist by any means whatever."

Petitions from individuals and groups of prisoners asking to take the oath of allegiance began as early as March, 1862,[83] and increased as rumors of a general exchange seeped through the camp. The writers suffered considerably from the resentment of their secessionist fellows, and one, who went so far as to write a pro-Union article for the *Journal,* found the prisoners particularly hot against him. A loyal Pennsylvanian was lodged for a time in the city jail on suspicion of being a spy. When it seemed probable to the authorities that he would be able to establish his standing as a Union man, they transferred him to the less uncomfortable camp to wait until the case was decided; soon they had to transfer him back, jail proving less unendurable than the jeers and taunts of the prisoners.

While Camp Morton was settling into comparative serenity, and good feeling grew between the prisoners and the authorities in this little backwater, the main current of war rolled heavily along. In May, 1862, Washington was thrown into a panic by the repeated thrusts of the Confederates, and Morton was called upon for more troops. Brigadier General G. W. Morgan was asking at the same time for troops to be used against John Morgan. On May 12 Governor Morton's secretary telegraphed Morgan that he had scarcely enough infantry to guard the prisoners. Ten days later he suggested to Stanton that if "the rebels" could be sent to Sandusky and Columbus, a good regiment would be ready for immediate service. This

[83] Petitions in Executive Department file, 109.9, 1861, Archives Division, Indiana State Library; Indianapolis *Journal,* March 11, 1862, p. 3, c. 2; March 12, p. 3, c. 1; March 27, p. 3, c. 1.

regiment was of course Owen's Sixtieth. On May 26 orders came for the regiment to be sent to Halleck, and calls were hurriedly sent out for companies of three-months men to guard Camp Morton.[84]

Colonel Hoffman hated to see the efficient organization at Indianapolis disturbed. He visited Camp Morton toward the end of May and expressed himself as highly pleased with the manner in which the prisoners were kept, and with the management of the finance, quartermaster's, and subsistence departments.[85] Although authorized to retain the commanders of Camps Douglas and Morton temporarily, he realized the objections to detaching a colonel from his regiment, and did not try to hold Owen, but he did ask that Lieutenant John J. Palmer, able post quartermaster at Camp Morton, be allowed to remain. Morton, far more interested in keeping the regiment intact, denied having authority to detail Palmer for such duty, and sent him along with Owen.[86]

The news that Owen had been ordered into active service was received by the prisoners with apprehension. There is some evidence that they thought his removal was hastened by the consideration he had shown them. They addressed the following petition to the Governor:[87]

"Knowing that it is a matter of state pride with your Excellency that prisoners of war sent to Indiana should remain quietly until satisfactory arrangements can be made for their release, and believing that this object can better be attained by the 60th regiment being retained in their present situation than by any change, we respectfully solicit your Excellency, if not

[84]Oliver P. Morton, Telegraphic Correspondence, February 5-June 10, 1862, pp. 240, 241, 243, 255, 259, 262, 263, 273, 274, 278, 279, 289.

[85]Indianapolis *Journal*, June 4, 1862, p. 3, c. 1.

[86]Lorenzo Thomas to Hoffman, June 13, 1862, *Official Records*, 2 series, IV, 15; Hoffman to Morton, June 26, 1862, in Sixtieth Regiment Indiana Volunteers file, folder A, Archives Division, Indiana State Library; Morton to Hoffman, June 28, 1862, in Morton Letter Book, June 23, 1862-January 17, 1863, pp. 21-22.

[87]Owen to Morton, May 29, 1862, Richard Owen file, Archives Division, Indiana State Library. The petition is printed in the Indianapolis *Journal*, May 31, 1862, p. 2, c. 1. The original is in the Oliver Perry Morton special file, Archives Division.

inconsistent with the interests to which you are pledged, that you will permit the same regiment still to remain in command of Camp Morton feeling that while true to their Government and strictly carrying out all the regulations of your Excellency, they have combined therewith the humanity and kindness we so highly appreciate. As an inducement to grant our request we pledge ourselves that we will conform to the prescribed rules and regulations adopted by your Excellency for our observation and safekeeping, and you will never have cause to repent your having granted us this favor."

The need for experienced troops outweighed any other consideration at the moment, and the only result of the petition was to put on record the devotion which Owen had inspired. He and his regiment left Indianapolis for Louisville on June 20.[88] They were sent to Lebanon, and from there to Munfordville, Kentucky. There, in September, the Union forces were surrounded by General Braxton Bragg's army, and Owen was captured with part of his regiment. His generosity to the Fort Donelson prisoners was promptly repaid. General Buckner, by this time exchanged and again in service, thanked the Colonel for his kindness to prisoners at Camp Morton and returned his side arms. The men of the Sixtieth Indiana were greeted with equal friendliness by their former prisoners and joined in the jokes on the vicissitudes of war.[89]

A further tribute from southern prisoners to Colonel Owen is the bronze bust in the main-floor corridor of the State House at Indianapolis. More than one memorial to this man exists, but only this one is connected with Camp Morton. S. A. Cunningham, for many years editor of the *Confederate Veteran*, conceived the idea,[90] and received permission in 1911 to place a bronze memorial tablet somewhere in Indianapolis. Contributions to the project were so generous that the bronze bust illustrated opposite page 262 was substituted for the tablet.

[88]Noble, A. G. O., Letter and Order Book No. 1, pp. 282, 287, 294.
[89]Indianapolis *Sentinel*, October 4, 1862, p. 3, c. 2; *Official Records*, 1 series, XIX, pt. 1, pp. 959 ff.; N. H. Winchell, *A Sketch of Richard Owen* (reprint from *American Geologist*, September, 1890), p. 137.
[90][Cunningham], *Memorials* . . ., pp. 1-31.

It was beautifully designed by Belle Kinney, daughter of a Confederate soldier, and bears a heartwarming inscription:

COLONEL RICHARD OWEN

COMMANDANT

CAMP MORTON PRISON 1862

Tribute by Confederate prisoners

of war and their friends

for his courtesy and kindness.

III. DAVID GARLAND ROSE: EXCHANGES AND PAROLES, 1862

CAMP MORTON was in a bustle of reorganization from the last week in May, 1862, until the middle of June. Like a magician suddenly called upon to pull a rabbit from a hat, Governor Morton was expected to provide a new commandant and to recruit, organize, muster in, and administer a little rudimentary training to a new force of guards.

His choice for commandant was David Garland Rose, United States marshal for Indiana since 1861. Rose had served as special aide to Morton in connection with relief work among soldiers in Missouri. Because there was some fear that his appointment as commandant at Camp Morton might vacate or interfere with his Federal office as marshal, the position of commandant was offered to Colonel John L. Mansfield of Jefferson County on June 7. Mansfield, engaged with General Love in organizing the Indiana Legion, declined. Morton then appealed to President Lincoln to arrange matters to permit Rose's appointment at Camp Morton. He was mustered in as colonel of the Fifty-fourth Indiana Volunteers, in charge of the camp, on June 19.[1] L. Gilbert Knox was appointed lieutenant colonel, and William C. Lupton post quartermaster.[2]

In the meantime, Adjutant General Noble had been busy assembling a guard from the Indiana Legion. General Orders No. 38, issued on May 28, 1862, asked for fifteen hundred men, organized in companies of not less than sixty-seven, for four-months service. They were to be mustered into United States service, and receive the same pay and allowance as United States volunteers. This order was superseded on June 2 by General Orders No. 41, which shortened the

[1]Terrell, *Report,* II, xi, 533; Morton, Telegraphic Correspondence, February 5-June 10, 1862, pp. 298, 308, 312; *ibid.,* June 11-July 31, 1862, pp. 14, 26.
[2]Terrell, *Report,* II, 533.

period of service and made some other modifications in the original order.[3]

Among the first replacements to reach Camp Morton were three Legion companies from Jefferson County. The men in one of these companies had volunteered unanimously, leaving their farms to look after themselves. Volunteers came from all sections of the state. By the end of the first week in June over four hundred had been sworn in for three-months service, and there were half as many more waiting for their companies to be completed. Some of the recruits went into the Fifty-fourth Regiment, under Colonel Rose, some into the Fifty-fifth, under Colonel John R. Mahan. Most of the Fifty-fourth remained at Camp Morton until August; seven companies of the Fifty-fifth were sent to Kentucky in July, and another call went out for replacements at the prisoners' camp. The new men were called for thirty days only.[4]

Continuous shifting of the guard companies caused some confusion at the camp. Lack of experience among the men caused more. They were unaccustomed to strict discipline; some of them were so awkward with firearms that they wounded themselves. Many of them worried about the fields left untended at home, and because a good harvest was important, they were allowed ten-day furloughs—in relays—to bring in the crops.[5]

Governor Morton, trying to supply troops for active service to meet the heavy demands in June and July, resented the tying up of more than a thousand men at Camp Morton, and telegraphed for permission to distribute the prisoners among the camps in Illinois and Ohio. He might have been allowed to

[3]Indianapolis *Sentinel,* May 31, 1862, p. 3, c. 1; June 3, p. 3, c. 2.

[4]Terrell, *Report,* I, 129, 131-34; *Report of Major-General Love, of the Indiana Legion,* 1861-62 (Indianapolis, 1863), pp. 6-7, 55, 57, 59; Morton, Telegraphic Correspondence, February 5-June 10, 1862, pp. 278, 290; *ibid.,* June 11-July 31, 1862, pp. 84-107 *passim,* 142; Madison *Courier* (daily), May 29, June 7, June 14, July 7, July 14, 1862; Indianapolis *Journal,* June 18, 1862, p. 3, c. 1; July 4, p. 3, c. 4; July 14, p. 3, c. 5; Indianapolis *Sentinel,* July 18, 1862, p. 3, c. 3.

[5]*Ibid.,* July 6, 1862, p. 3, c. 1; Noble, A. G. O., Letter and Order Book No. 1, p. 348.

do this had not the plans for a general exchange intervened.[6]

Under Colonel Rose, a cold militarism gradually supplanted the paternalistic camp administration which had been cultivated by Owen. Some of the prisoners disliked the new commandant intensely, and in after years had a tendency to attribute to Owen's regime any pleasant occurrence at Camp Morton. For example, the following incident, which, if it happened at all, happened after Rose took charge, was related in the *Confederate Veteran* as evidence of Owen's magnanimity. On July 3, 1862, a canard spread through central Indiana that McClellan had gained a great victory, that Lee's army was routed, and that Federal troops were in possession of Richmond. There was great rejoicing in Indianapolis—illuminations, speechmaking, and vociferous cheering. The prisoners were well aware of the celebration. Next day the truth came out—Richmond was still in Confederate hands, and McClellan had fallen back. That night all the little candle ends in camp—prisoners were allowed to use them until taps—twinkled from stumps of trees and every conspicuous spot in the enclosure. But there was no speechmaking or cheering, and voices were kept down to the level of a whisper. When taps was sounded, every light was extinguished promptly. Some good citizens protested at this unrepentant display, but the Commandant in this instance upheld the prisoners.[7]

Rose wished to take under advisement with Colonel Hoffman some special cases among the prisoners, and also the handling of the prisoners' fund. He wrote to Hoffman on July 4, asking him to visit the camp.[8] Hoffman's headquarters had by this time been transferred to Detroit, and he had been given full supervision of prisoners of war sent by generals in the field to prison camps.[9] On the seventh of July he issued

[6]Morton, Telegraphic Correspondence, June 11-July 31, 1862, pp. 52, 58, 64.

[7]Evander Shapard, "Recollections of Camp Morton," in *Confederate Veteran*, VIII, 211 (May, 1900); *ibid.*, XIV, 394 (September, 1906); XV, 203 (May, 1907); Indianapolis *Sentinel*, July 3, 1862, p. 3, c. 5; July 4, p. 3, c. 5.

[8]*Official Records*, 2 series, IV, 126.

[9]He was expected to visit the camps once a month, if practicable. General Orders No. 67, July 17, 1862, *ibid.*, IV, 30.

a set of regulations to all prison camp commandants, which is interesting in comparison with the rules formulated by Owen.[10]

"The following regulations will be observed at all stations where prisoners of war are held:

"1. The commanding officer at each station is held accountable for the discipline and good order of his command and for the security of the prisoners, and will take such measures as will best secure these results. He will divide the prisoners into companies, and will cause written reports to be made to him of their condition every morning showing the changes made during the preceding twenty-four hours, giving the names of the 'joined,' 'transferred,' 'deaths,' &c. At the end of every month commanders will send to the commissary-general of prisoners a return of prisoners, giving names and details to explain alterations. Where rolls of 'joined' or 'transferred' have been forwarded during the month it will be sufficient to refer to them on the return.

"2. On the arrival of prisoners at any station a careful comparison of them with the rolls that accompany them will be made and all errors on the rolls will be corrected. When no roll accompanies the prisoners one will be immediately made out containing all the information required as correct as can be from the statements of the prisoners themselves. When the prisoners are citizens the town, county, and State from which they come will be given on the rolls under the heads, rank, regiment and company. At the same time they will be required to give up all arms and weapons of every description and all moneys which they have in their possession, for which the commanding officer will give receipts.

"3. The hospital will be under the immediate charge of the senior surgeon who will be held responsible to the commanding officer for its good order and the condition of the sick. 'The fund' of this hospital will be kept separate from the fund of the hospital for the troops and will be disbursed for the sole benefit of the sick prisoners on the requisition of the surgeon approved by the commanding officer. When the fund is sufficiently large there will be bought with it besides

[10] *Ibid.*, IV, 152-53.

the articles usually purchased all articles of table furniture, kitchen utensils, articles for policing, shirts and drawers for the sick, the expense of washing, and all articles that may be indispensably necessary to promote the sanitary condition of the hospital.

"4. The commanding officer will cause requisitions to be made by his quartermaster on the nearest depot for such clothing as may be absolutely necessary for the prisoners, which requisition will be approved by him after a careful inquiry as to the necessity and submitted for the approval of the commissary-general of prisoners. The clothing will be issued by the quartermaster to the prisoners with the assistance and under the supervision of an officer detailed for the purpose, whose certificate that the issue has been made in his presence will be the quartermaster's voucher for the clothing issued. From the 30th of April to the 1st of October neither drawers nor socks will be allowed except to the sick.

"5. A general fund for the benefit of the prisoners will be made by withholding from their rations all that can be spared without inconvenience to them, and selling this surplus under existing regulations to the commissary, who will hold the funds in his hands and be accountable for them subject to the commanding officer's order to cover purchases. The purchases with the fund will be made by or through the quartermaster with the approval or order of the commanding officer, the bills being paid by the commissary, who will keep an account book in which will be carefully entered all receipts and payments with the vouchers; and he will keep the commanding officer advised from time to time of the amount of this fund. At the end of the month he will furnish the commanding officer with an account of the fund for the month showing the receipts and disbursements, which account will be forwarded to the commissary-general of prisoners with the remarks of the commanding officer. With this fund will be purchased all such articles as may be necessary for the health and comfort of the prisoners and which would otherwise have to be purchased by the Government. Among these articles are all table furniture and cooking utensils, articles for policing purposes, bedticks and straw, the means of improving or enlarging the barrack accommodations, extra pay to clerks who have charge of the camp post-office, and who keep the accounts of moneys deposited with the commanding officer, &c., &c.

"6. The sutler is entirely under the control of the commanding officer who will see that he furnishes proper articles, and at reasonable rates. For his privilege the sutler will be taxed a small amount by the commanding officer according to the amount of his trade, which tax will make a part of the general fund.

"7. Prisoners will not be permitted to hold or receive money. All moneys in possession or received will be taken charge of by the commanding officer who will give receipts for it to those to whom it belongs. They will purchase from the sutler such articles as they may wish, which are not prohibited, and on the bill of the articles they will give an order on the commanding officer for the amount, and this will be kept as a voucher with the individual's account. The commanding officer will keep a book in which the accounts of all those who have money deposited with him will be kept, and this book with the vouchers must be always ready for the inspection of the commissary-general of prisoners.

"8. All articles contributed by friends for the prisoners in whatever shape they come if proper to be received will be carefully distributed as the donors may request; such articles as are intended for the sick passing through the hands of the surgeon who will be responsible for their proper use. Contributions must be received by an officer who must be held responsible that they are delivered to the persons for whom they are intended.

"9. Visitors to these stations out of mere curiosity will in no case be permitted. Persons having business with the commanding officer or quartermaster may with the permission of the commanding officer enter the camp to remain only long enough to transact their business. When prisoners are seriously ill their nearest relatives, parents, wives, brothers or sisters if they are loyal people may be permitted to make them short visits; but under no other circumstances will visitors be allowed to see them without the approval of the commissary-general of prisoners.

"10. Prisoners will not be permitted to write letters of more than one page of common letter paper, the matter to be strictly of a private nature, or the letter must be destroyed.

"11. Prisoners will be paroled or released only by the authority of the War Department, or by direction of the commissary-general of prisoners."

In Rule 5, Rose found the answer to his uncertainties about the handling of the prisoners' fund. It did away with the self-constituted council at Camp Morton which had heretofore ordered expenditures, and to which Quartermaster Ekin had objected; responsibility was now concentrated in the hands of Ekin and the commandant. After a visit to the camp, Hoffman gave Rose further explicit directions. The post quartermaster and commissary, Lieutenant Lupton, was to make no purchases himself. As treasurer of the fund, he was to pay only bills made in Captain Ekin's name, and approved by Rose. Certain post expenditures were criticized—too much for postage and tobacco, and not enough for vegetables; improper payments in connection with the pursuit of escaped prisoners; too much pay to employees at the camp; the engagement of a civilian as paymaster at fifty dollars a month. The necessity of keeping the accounts and rolls up-to-date was emphasized once more.[11]

Toward the middle of July a stampede among the prisoners startled the town. First rumors had it that a hundred prisoners had escaped and fifteen or twenty had been killed; Captain Ekin telegraphed Secretary Stanton that fifty had escaped; but the *Journal*, after investigating at Camp Morton and the hospitals, set the number at about twenty-five. The removal of one of the more experienced guard regiments and the stormy, rainy night of July 14 gave the prisoners as good a chance for escape as they could ever hope for. Prying loose the posts at the northeast corner of the enclosure, they rushed the fence and forced a few panels. The guards, alarmed by the commotion, beat the long roll, and Colonel Rose hastily ordered out all

[11] *Official Records,* 2 series, IV, 240-41.

available men in three pursuit parties, one along the pike to the left, one to the right, and one to sweep the area between. Thirteen of the fleeing men, two of them wounded, were captured within twenty-four hours; one poor soul got "tired of walking" and surrendered to a conductor on the Terre Haute line; all the rest but one were brought back to the camp by July 18.[12]

In spite of the stringent orders to prevent prisoners from approaching the walls, some of the more desperate men in the camp continued to take chances by obeying orders tardily or not at all. On July 24 one of this group was wounded by a guard who had apparently given the required three warnings and then fired. The case was reviewed by a court of inquiry, and the guard's action sustained.[13]

Disturbing to the morale of the camp as these occurrences were, their effect was minimized by the great excitement following rumors of a general exchange of prisoners.[14] The subject had been under discussion between Union and Confederate officials for months, but a cartel of exchange was not signed until July 22.[15] Even after the signing, the success of negotiations was threatened in various ways. For example, Governor John Letcher, of Virginia, infuriated by General Pope's order for the removal of disloyal citizens from their lands in the rear of his lines, claimed from the War Department of the Confederacy the right to try Union officers captured in Virginia in the state courts, on charges of treason and inciting slaves to insurrection.[16] The actual exchange did not take place until late in August.

[12]Indianapolis *Journal*, July 16, 1862, p. 3, c. 2; July 17, p. 3, c. 1; July 18, p. 3, c. 2; Indianapolis *Sentinel*, July 16, 1862, p. 3, c. 1; July 18, p. 3, c. 1; *Official Records*, 2 series, IV, 225.

[13]Indianapolis *Sentinel*, July 25, 1862, p. 3, c. 1; Indianapolis *Journal*, July 26, 1862, p. 3, c. 3.

[14]Indianapolis *Sentinel*, June 17, 1862, p. 3, c. 2.

[15]Hesseltine, *Civil War Prisons*, 17-33.

[16]*Ibid.*, 71, 74, 89; *Official Records*, 2 series, IV, 781, 828-29, 849-50, 875-76; V, 147-48, 212, 222, 223, 286, 358. It was not until March, 1863, that the Virginia legislature overruled the Governor and transferred to the Confederate Government the whole problem of prisoners. See also Indianapolis *Journal*, August 15, 1862, p. 2, c. 1; Indianapolis *Sentinel*, August 16, 1862, p. 2, c. 1.

All through the months of June and July Camp Morton buzzed with surmises as to where and when the exchange would take place. Another question was raised by some of the prisoners. What would happen if a man didn't want to be exchanged? Some men felt that they had made a mistake in enlisting; some were influenced by the fact that in the North good labor was in demand and wages were high; others, whom public opinion had forced into service, dreaded the thought of an exchange which would make them liable for further service.

This attitude was particularly strong among the Tennesseans. Owen, a few days before his departure, wrote to Ekin:[17] "After the reception at Camp Morton of a letter addressed by the War Department to a prisoner named Williams, indicating that negotiations were pending for an exchange of prisoners, many persons individually & also as delegates from whole companies, especially of Tennesseans, stated verbally & also in writing, that they should *not* like to be exchanged. Some of them said they would rather remain in Camp Morton than be exchanged; others enquired if there was no mode whatever by which they could hope to see their homes again except by being forced into the southern army again, which they earnestly desired to avoid.

"Judging from all I have seen and heard since the 20th day of Feb. /62 when I took charge of the prisoners of war at Camp Morton, I think I am justified in the belief that at least two thirds of the men from Tennessee . . . would regret any circumstances which induced or compelled them again to take up arms against the Union."

Ekin transmitted Owen's letter to the Secretary of War, with his own endorsement of the views expressed. Assurance came back from Washington that when a system of exchange had been established, no prisoners whose loyalty to the Union was unquestioned would be "forced within the rebel lines."[18] On August 2, Ekin addressed Stanton again, asking what rule

[17]Letter of June 17, 1862, enclosed with Ekin's letter of the same date to Secretary of War Stanton. Photostat in Indiana Division, Indiana State Library.

[18]C. P. Wolcott to Owen, June 21, 1862, *Official Records,* 2 series, IV, 48. See also *ibid.,* IV, 328.

was to be adopted in the case of the prisoners at Camp Morton who wanted to take the oath of allegiance.[19]

Most of Tennessee was at this time in Union hands, and a temporary government had been set up with Andrew Johnson as military governor. He was asked by the War Department for suggestions as to the disposition of the Tennesseans at Camp Morton, and proposed that a commissioner be sent to examine all Tennesseans in northern prison camps. Those willing to take the oath and meaning it, would be released; those unwilling to comply or whose motives were questionable would be held for exchange or continued confinement.[20]

Johnson's plan was carried out. Former Governor William B. Campbell, the commissioner appointed, reached Indianapolis on the thirteenth of August and began his examination of the prisoners.[21] The camp was in a turmoil. Prisoners wishing to take the oath were marched outside the enclosure for the ceremony. According to the *Sentinel*,[22] those inside "hooted, yelled, threw stones, old shoes, and every missile they could lay their hands on, at the peaceably-disposed. Col. Rose had patrols placed over the ground to keep order, and was obliged to threaten the free use of powder and ball. One prisoner insisted upon mounting the fence. The guard outside ordered him down. He would not get down. The guard then fired over his head. At this the man only evinced the greater determination to keep his head above the fence. The guard then deliberately fired at him. The ball passed through the ear of the man aimed at, and struck one on the inside, some fifty or one hundred yards away, in the forehead, killing him instantly."

[19]*Ibid.,* IV, 331. See also Hoffman to General Thomas, July 15, 1862, *ibid.,* IV, 223.

[20]*Ibid.,* IV, 328, 333. Johnson had had the matter under consideration for some time. In April, Tennessee prisoners at Camp Douglas had appealed to him to use his influence with the Federal Government to secure their release upon taking the oath of allegiance. At that time Johnson wrote to Secretary Stanton that he thought the reappearance of the prisoners among their friends and relatives would "exert a great moral influence in favor of the perpetuity of the Union." *Ibid.,* III, 457-58, 643.

[21]*Ibid.,* IV, 362, 387.

[22]Indianapolis *Sentinel,* August 16, 1862, p. 3, c. 1, 2; Indianapolis *Journal,* August 16, 1862, p. 3, c. 2.

Although order was restored without further bloodshed, Ekin telegraphed for permission to remove the Union sympathizers, because the feelings of the other prisoners were so bitter toward them. He was instructed to hold them until Adjutant General Thomas should arrive with instructions. On the twentieth Thomas and Colonel Hoffman both reached Indianapolis, where they interviewed Governor Morton and Campbell, and it was arranged that the prisoners from Tennessee who had taken the oath should be released and furnished transportation to Nashville. Most of them left Indianapolis on August 22, six months almost to the day from their entry to Camp Morton. Over three hundred had taken the oath of allegiance.[23]

During his visit, General Thomas made a thorough examination of Camp Morton, and of the other camps and the arsenal. The administration of the Camp Morton quartermaster's and commissary departments he complimented as the best seen in any prison camp.[24] Thomas' principal concern was the completion of arrangements for exchange, which he worked out with Hoffman and the camp authorities. There was the question of guards. By this time two-thirds of the force at the camp were thirty-day men, whose time of service had expired on August 17. Willing to do their share in the emergency, most of these men agreed to remain until the exchange had been completed.[25]

Rolls of all prisoners, including those on parole, had already been made up under an order issued by Hoffman to camp commandants on July 31.[26] Hoffman had never ceased exhorting his subordinates to keep their records straight, but now every slip, every omission, every error that had been made was vitally important to some prisoner. A man could not be exchanged if his name did not show on both Union and Confederate tallies. If he had enlisted under a false name and forgotten his pseudonym or if his name had been struck off the rolls by

[23]*Official Records,* 2 series, IV, 396, 397, 410, 413-14, 422. Indianapolis *Journal,* August 22, 1862, p. 3, c. 1; August 23, p. 3, c. 1.

[24]Indianapolis *Sentinel,* August 22, 1862, p. 3, c. 2.

[25]*Official Records,* 2 series, IV, 331, 361, 375.

[26]*Ibid.,* IV, 318-19.

mischance, he was liable to be classed with the guerilla prisoners, who were recognized by neither government and were not subject to exchange.[27]

Death rolls were neither complete nor accurate, and some guerillas managed to be exchanged by answering to the names of dead men from organized regiments.[28] In spite of the care exercised slip-ups did occur, some too ludicrous to be received as sober fact. For example, there was the famous case, not connected with Camp Morton, of Lieutenant J. W. Adams, who was exchanged three times, all without his knowledge and while he was flat on his back in a hospital at West Point.[29]

Final orders for the removal of the prisoners were issued on August 22. Captain H. M. Lazelle, Eighth United States Infantry, was made agent for their delivery at Vicksburg; Captain H. W. Freedley, Third United States Infantry, superintended their departure from Camp Morton. To Lazelle, Hoffman wrote:[30]

"The prisoners of war at Camp Morton will be forwarded to Cairo by rail and thence on steamers to Vicksburg under a flag of truce. They will leave in three detachments—the first to-morrow evening. . . .

"Each party will take with them rations for the day on which they will leave. . . .

"A guard of one company will be provided by the commander of Camp Morton to accompany each party. The three parties will be assembled at Cairo whence they will leave at the same time on steamboats under convoy, the whole being under your orders.

"The commanding officer at Cairo has been instructed to furnish all things that may be necessary for the movement.

"All moneys belonging to prisoners in the hands of Colonel Rose will be turned over to you with a detailed account of the amount due each person, and the amount will be given to the prisoners by you when they are turned over to the Confederate agent.

[27]*Ibid.*, IV, 437.
[28]*Ibid.*, IV, 545.
[29]*Ibid.*, IV, 474.
[30]*Ibid.*, IV, 420-21.

"You will be furnished with duplicate rolls of all prisoners to be exchanged, and when they are delivered to the agent of the Confederate States you will take his receipt on both rolls for all prisoners present, one of the rolls being left in his hands and the other you will forward to the Adjutant General at Washington."

Freedley received some additional instructions.[31] Guerilla prisoners and political prisoners were to be sent to the depot at Sandusky. The account of the prisoners' fund was to be made up as soon as possible and sent to Hoffman at Detroit. To help in this business, Hoffman allowed the retention of prisoners of war who were acting as clerks in the quartermaster's department, with the understanding that they be sent to Cairo before September 15.

Twelve hundred thirty-eight prisoners left Indianapolis on Saturday, August 23, departing as they had arrived, among a crowd of interested spectators; 773 more left for Cairo on Sunday, 333 for Sandusky on Monday, and 990 for Cairo on Wednesday. One lot of prisoners, probably about six hundred, was scheduled to leave for Cairo Thursday.[32] Safely southbound from Cairo on the gunboat "Lexington," the prisoners began to worry about the arms which had been taken from them at Camp Morton and, to the probable confusion of Captain Lazelle, produced a receipt for them from the camp commandant. It is probable that they did receive their worn and blunted knives, but their pistols were lost to them forever. Orders directing the return of "side arms" to the Fort Donelson prisoners upon their arrival at Vicksburg had expressly excluded that weapon.[33] There remained at Camp Morton a few men whose names did not appear on any rolls—among them a group of 26 from Kentucky who had just arrived—and in the City Hospital, another group of the sick and their nurses, 107 in number. The greater part of the

[31] *Official Records,* 2 series, IV, 421.
[32] *Ibid.,* IV, 436-37, 460-61; Indianapolis *Journal,* August 25, 1862, p. 3, c. 2; August 28, p. 3, c. 2; August 29, p. 3, c. 3; September 1, p. 3, c. 3; Indianapolis *Sentinel,* August 25, 1862, p. 3, c. 2; August 27, p. 3, c. 1.
[33] *Official Records,* 2 series, IV, 365, 464, 521.

convalescents were discharged in the first week of September.[34]
The actual exchange of prisoners at Vicksburg was in
charge of two field officers, one Union, one Confederate.
These officers had the right to refuse to accept any man whose
organization they did not recognize, or any man whom they
knew to be a criminal with warrants out against him. The
following table of equivalents had been agreed upon in the
cartel drawn up by General John A. Dix of the Union Army
and General Daniel H. Hill, for the Confederacy:[35]

Commander in Chief or Admiral	for officer of equal rank	or	60	privates or common seamen
Flag officer or Major General	"	"	40	"
Commodore or Brig-adier General	"	"	20	"
Navy Captain or Colonel	"	"	15	"
Commander or Lieut. Col.	"	"	10	"
Lieut. Commander or Major	"	"	8	"
Navy Lieut. or Army Captain	"	"	6	"
Master's Mate or Army Lieut. or Ensign	"	"	4	"
Midshipman, navy warrant officer, master of mer-chant vessel, or commander of pri-vateer	"	"	3	"
All petty officers or noncoms.	"	"	2	"

The men to be exchanged stood in two lines, Indian file, the
line of Confederates headed south, the Federal men headed
north. This apparently childish arrangement added a great
deal to the moral effect of the exchange. At a certain spot

[34]*Ibid.*, IV, 461; Indianapolis *Journal*, September 3, 1862, p. 3, c. 2;
Noble, A. G. O., Letter and Order Book No. 1, p. 479.
[35]*Official Records*, 2 series, IV, 266-67.

some distance from any building, ditch, or tree, two captains, one Union, the other Confederate, stood facing each other. Ten feet away stood another pair of captains. The Union men moved north between one pair of captains, the Confederates moved south between the other pair. As each prisoner passed between the officers, each captain struck him lightly on the shoulder, counting audibly—one, two, three, and so on. Each captain had to have the table of exchange clearly in mind, and watch for the insignia of rank. After the count of "fifty" the lines halted. A sergeant's guard from each side stood by to see to it that the fifty men who had just been counted stood in the line until the count had been verified, and that the fifty men in each line were agreed upon by the two captains in each case. The trouble came, of course, from the fact that there were not always fifty men in the line, but the equivalent of the number, according to the table adopted.

When both lines had been checked, the men could break rank and join their friends, but these groups had to be unarmed, and were not permitted to approach within one hundred feet of the four officers who did the counting. The counting was a slow and tiresome process, since many of the men were ill and had to be helped. Many of them were overcome with emotion; some fainted from exhaustion. Everyone was eager to get the matter over with and everything possible was done to expedite the exchange.[36]

Following the actual exchange, each government took charge of its own reclaimed men. After a physical examination, those who were fit were returned to their own outfits or assigned to others. Those whose health was impaired were sent home on furlough or discharged. Some who were not equal to duty in the field were put to such lighter work as orderly service or guard duty in public buildings. Their main requirements were plenty of sleep and shelter from bad weather. Many of this class eventually made a complete recovery.

[36]From a verbal account given by the late Captain and Assistant Adjutant General E. Lewis Moore, Seventh Connecticut Volunteers, who served as an official several times during exchange.

The closing of prison camp records at Camp Morton fell to Captain Freedley. Any part of the prisoners' fund remaining on hand was to be turned over to Captain Thomas Foster, Jr., commissary of subsistence at Indianapolis. Sums of money belonging to prisoners and uncalled for at their departure were to be turned over to Hoffman, with a list of the owners. The rolls for the last two months and a half had to be checked and put in order. All this done, the records of the camp were to be safely boxed and put into the hands of Captain Ekin.[37]

By the first of September, 1862, Camp Morton had been cleared of rebel prisoners. It was in bad shape, and an immediate "renovation and purification" was begun by companies from the Fifth Cavalry. They had instructions to put the quarters into shape and build new bunks,[38] but before much work could be done, accommodations were required for troops in training and for Indiana volunteers who had been captured at Richmond, Kentucky, on August 30, and sent home on parole. On Saturday morning, September 6, the State House grove was crowded with men from the Twelfth, Sixteenth, and Fifty-fifth Indiana Regiments, the first arrivals. After some delay they were organized as far as possible into their regular companies, and marched out to Camp Morton.[39] Several thousand more Indiana troops, including Colonel Owen and part of the Sixtieth, were paroled at Munfordville, Kentucky, on September 17. They were not allowed to take their way northward through the Confederate lines, but sent southward with four days rations, to reach the Union forces under Buell at Bowling Green and then make their way to Louisville. From there some of them were sent to Indianapolis.[40]

The War Department had set up camps of instruction for paroled prisoners, one at Annapolis, one at Camp Chase, one in Missouri. Indiana prisoners were scheduled to go to Camp Chase. Morton combated this arrangement with his usual extraordinary vigor, for parolees there were said to be badly

[37]*Official Records*, 2 series, IV, 567.

[38]Indianapolis *Sentinel*, August 26, 1862, p. 3, c. 1; September 4, p. 3, c. 1; Noble, A. G. O., Letter and Order Book No. 1, p. 477.

[39]Indianapolis *Journal*, September 8, 1862, p. 3, c. 1.

[40]*Official Records*, 2 series, IV, 701.

demoralized—insubordinate, indifferent, and disinclined to make any effort to fit themselves for further service.[41] The Governor had no intention of allowing the same thing to happen to six thousand Indianans. He was determined to keep them in their own state, maintain discipline, and give them intensive training toward the time when exchange would make them available in the field.[42]

Two things worked in Morton's favor. First, the commandant at Camp Chase begged that no more paroled prisoners be sent there.[43] Second, a twenty-day furlough was granted to officers and men of several of the captured Indiana regiments.[44] They were ordered to report at Camp Chase on October 21, but Morton was rightly confident that he could keep them in Indiana.

Apparently the Twelfth and Sixteenth Regiments remained at Camp Morton, which was put in charge of Colonel John R. Mahan.[45] The Fifty-fifth was mustered out toward the middle of September when its term of enlistment expired. Parts of other paroled regiments may have remained, and at least one regiment of recruits (the One Hundredth) was in training during September and October.

Letters written by the young adjutant of the One Hundredth Regiment give some idea of how the camp appeared to a recruit.[46] His regiment found it "in a very filthy condition," and had "lots of work to do to set things right," but in spite of cold nights, quarters with three others in a "very small and leaky shanty," and "none too much to eat," he liked the life "very well," and considered the men "happy and contented." On September 12, he reported that about fifteen hundred paroled prisoners from the Richmond fight were expected, and two weeks later wrote that times were lively with over three thousand troops in camp. His first review,

[41]*Official Records*, 2 series, IV, 94, 519, 546, 569-71, 594, 644-45.

[42]*Ibid.*, IV, 522, 562, 623, 638, 641; Morton, Telegraphic Correspondence, September 2-September 29, 1862, p. 314.

[43]*Official Records*, 2 series, IV, 563.

[44]*Ibid.*, IV, 571, 572, 585-86, 613.

[45]Indianapolis *Journal*, November 13, 1862, p. 3, c. 1.

[46]Edward P. Williams, *Extracts from Letters . . . 1862-1864* (New York, 1903), pp. 5-14. See also Indianapolis *Journal*, November 13, 1862, p. 3, c. 1.

which kept him in the saddle for two hours in the forenoon and from one until six-thirty in the afternoon, left him "very tired," but he had worn his full dress uniform, "the first occasion," and considered the day a satisfactory one.

Nothing really bothered him except the Sundays. "There was preaching this evening," he wrote on October 5, "but none during the day, the men having been kept busy cleaning up the whole grounds. The whole camp (thirty acres) was swept thoroughly. I do not approve of making the men do so much work on Sunday." And later: "Am sorry to say we know no Sunday here. It is hard work every day. Never in all my life has time passed so rapidly as here."

Late in the month three thousand paroled prisoners came into camp at the end of their furloughs, and from that time there was a good deal of trouble in holding in check the more rebellious of them. Such compensations as the recruits discovered in the hard, driving days at Camp Morton made little appeal to the paroled men. They were tired and their morale was low. Having lost most of their belongings in Kentucky, they expected a fresh issue of tents and mess equipment, but discovered that the Government did not provide these things for paroled soldiers.

They wrote bitterly to the newspapers[47] that they had been ordered to camp "to drill, to be rearmed and reclothed and await exchange," but actually had "barely escaped starving." Their whole treatment seemed to be of a "uniform meanness," which they interpreted as punishment for a capture which was not their fault. It was a specially sore point that the camp of the drafted men was filled with tents while they were left to manage as best they might.

Although they were not permitted to do any duty which would free troops for active service, they were kept busy guarding and policing their own camp, repairing barracks required for their own use, drilling seven hours a day, and taking part in occasional parades.[48] This strict discipline had good results, and when word reached Indianapolis on November

[47]Indianapolis *Journal,* October 2, 1862, p. 3, c. 4; October 22, p. 3, c. 2.

[48]*Official Records,* 2 series, IV, 653-54. Colonel Henry B. Carrington had charge of the training.

17, 1862, that their exchange had at last been effected, the men were in excellent condition. It was a gala day at Camp Morton. The men cheered and shouted, and welcomed the Governor with enthusiasm when he arrived to address the regiments one by one.

Freed for service, the regiments began moving to the field as fast as organization and equipment were completed. There were still enough soldiers in town to make a good showing at the Thanksgiving Day celebration, but by December 6, Camp Morton was almost depopulated.[49]

[49]*Official Records,* 2 series, IV, 700-1, 705, 707, 717, 735-36; Indianapolis *Journal,* November 18, 1862, p. 3, c. 1; November 27, p. 3, c. 2; December 6, p. 3, c. 1.

IV. EMERGENCY HOSPITALS, 1862

MORE than one half of the Fort Donelson prisoners were in need of medical care when they reached Indianapolis late in February, 1862. The Mississippians were in particularly bad shape. In the retreat from Fort Henry they had lost most of their baggage and extra clothing; when they reached Fort Donelson they were at once pressed into work on the fortifications, and during the siege lay half frozen in the ditches and rifle pits day and night. Such exposure would have been dangerous to seasoned troops; among these lads, many of them under eighteen years of age, the effects were disastrous. The miserable journey to Indianapolis in the most disagreeable month of the year exhausted what little endurance they had left, and for the first six weeks after their arrival hundreds of them were on the sick list.[1]

Hospital quarters in the old power hall at Camp Morton were totally inadequate. Part of the small space was needed for guards on the sick list, leaving only twenty-five bunks for prisoners. At the City Hospital most of the beds were already occupied by sick and wounded Union soldiers, but some emergency cases among the prisoners were taken there.[2] Dr. Patrick H. Jameson treated as many as he could in the barracks at camp, with some assistance from prisoners who had a little medical knowledge. To provide for the rest, Adjutant General Noble, Quartermaster Ekin, and Dr. John S. Bobbs, chief surgeon, secured quarters in two buildings on Meridian Street.

One of these, the Gymnasium building on the northeast corner of Meridian and Maryland, became Military Hospital No. 2 almost overnight. About sixty prisoners were moved in on the twenty-sixth of February, and by March 3 the

[1]Indianapolis *Journal*, March 4, 1862, p. 3, c. 3; Patrick H. Jameson, Report to the Adjutant General, June 1, 1862, Executive Department file, 109.9, 1861, Archives Division, Indiana State Library.

[2]Indianapolis *Journal*, February 28, 1862, p. 3, c. 1.

number was more than doubled. The Reverend Horace Stringfellow, rector of Christ's Church, seems to have superintended the nursing during the first few days, aided by volunteers from the men and women of Indianapolis.[3]

In this little interval, good will sometimes had to take the place of training and experience. A story which went the rounds of the newspapers in the state illustrates this point, and is not past believing. Its central figure is a warmhearted young lady who had offered her services in the hospital, but found herself uncertain as to how best to make herself useful. At last, after several unsuccessful attempts to minister to the patients, she seized a towel and a basin of water and advanced upon another soldier. "Can't I wash your feet?" she asked. The man opened his eyes just long enough to reply with resignation, "Well, I don't care if it will be any pleasure to you, but they have already been washed three times today."

To bring some order out of the existing confusion, Dr. William B. Fletcher was put in charge of Hospital No. 2, and Colonel Owen was asked to send ten "sprightly intelligent" men from among the prisoners at Camp Morton to help with the sick. A few days later twenty more were called for. When about half of them proved "entirely worthless" as nurses, Adjutant General Noble asked Owen to supply eight or ten healthy Germans or Irishmen if they could be found. At the same time, "owing to the difficulty in properly organizing and arranging the Hospital," he issued an order excluding all visitors except those detailed for duty by the surgeon in charge. This rule was later extended to cover all the hospitals, and proved most beneficial. By March 6 Hospital No. 2 was functioning in an orderly way. Two matrons had been employed and kitchen accommodations improvised where food could be prepared properly. Already the capacity of the hospital was overtaxed, and again measures had been taken to secure supplementary quarters.[4]

[3] Indianapolis *Journal,* February 25, 1862, p. 3, c. 3; February 28, p. 3, c. 1; March 1, p. 3, c. 2. John H. Holliday, *Indianapolis and the Civil War* (Indiana Historical Society *Publications,* IV, no. 9, Indianapolis, 1911), 573.

[4] Noble, A. G. O., Letter and Order Book No. 1, pp. 146, 147, 152; Indianapolis *Journal,* March 4, 1862, p. 3, c. 4; March 6, p. 3, c. 2. Newspapers often referred to Hospital No. 2 as the Meridian Street Hospital.

Space was available in the old four-story post office on Meridian Street near the corner of Washington. Captain Ekin cut more red tape, contracted for the building on March 5, and had Military Hospital No. 3 crudely ready for patients in thirty-six hours. The first and second floors were divided into two wards each, and preparations were made for similar arrangement of the two upper stories. It was thought that from 200 to 250 men could be accommodated. Having no mattresses ready, Ekin begged help of the young ladies of Miss Merrill's school, and these young women put together one hundred and fifty bed sacks and a number of pillow slips in a single day. Dr. Talbot Bullard was placed in charge of this hospital, with Dr. Will Bullard as his assistant. Two sergeants from the Fourth Mississippi were selected as ward masters, and given a detail of twenty of their comrades to act as nurses. At least a hundred prisoners were brought into the hospital by March 7.[5]

In a few cases, sick prisoners were removed to private houses, where they could be cared for to better advantage than in crowded hospitals, but this practice was soon discontinued by General Halleck's orders.[6]

During these busy days, Colonel Hoffman, commissary general of prisoners, visited Camp Morton and the hospitals, and on March 5 reported to General Meigs what had been done.[7] Since the City Hospital, under Dr. Kitchen, was occupied exclusively by sick volunteers and prisoners of war, he arranged that expenses there be borne by the Government. Expenses of the two downtown hospitals were estimated at $225 each per month, exclusive of rent. At each the attending physician was paid $100, a steward, $40, two matrons, $30 each, and an apothecary, $25. Rental for one building was $104 and for the other, $60.

Supplies of sheets and pillowcases, and sufficient underclothing to insure cleanliness were authorized by the Government, but it took time to secure them in quantity, and appeals

[5]Indianapolis *Journal*, March 6, 1862, p. 3, c. 2; March 7, p. 3, c. 2. This hospital was often referred to as Center Hospital.

[6]Terrell, *Report*, I, 461-62; Indianapolis *Journal*, March 6, 1862, p. 3, c. 1; March 27, p. 3, c. 2.

[7]*Official Records*, 2 series, III, 348-49, 375.

were made to the townspeople to send old shirts, underclothing, and bed linen. Some homes were practically stripped of bedding, first, by contributions to sick Union soldiers in Kentucky and Indiana, and now by gifts to the prisoners. Their woeful state probably induced more than one young lady to give up her own pillow, when every spare one in the house had gone for some soldier's use.[8]

To secure suitable food for the sick men, a hospital fund was set up; this operated as did the prisoners' fund at Camp Morton. From the regular issue of one soldier's ration for each patient, excess quantities of food were bought back by the commissary, and the money thus accruing was expended in purchasing vegetables and delicacies. Here again the citizens of Indianapolis were asked to supplement what the hospital kitchens could supply. Corn bread and buttermilk were two of the articles most in demand, and quantities were sent in by individuals and associations. Clothing, fruits, and wines came also from friends of the prisoners in Kentucky. Additional purchases were made from the prisoners' fund, which increased much faster than the hospital fund.[9]

The improvised accommodations for the sick were far from satisfactory. Occupants of the building adjoining Hospital No. 2 objected to its location, protesting that the stench would be intolerable as summer months approached. A sharp reply in the *Journal* asserted that the hospital wards were clean, dry, and free from odor, and pointed out that the authorities had done the best they could in the exigencies of the situation: no quarters had been available outside the city, and the sick could not wait.[10]

The criticism was valid, however. The situation of the hospitals was not only bad for neighboring buildings; the dust and noise were undesirable for the patients. The buildings

[8]*Official Records,* 2 series, III, 375, 400-1; Indianapolis *Journal,* February 28, 1862, p. 3, c. 1; March 11, p. 3, c. 3; *Indiana Soldier,* I, 323-24.

[9]*Official Records,* 2 series, III, 401, 617, 620-21; Indianapolis *Journal,* March 5, 1862, p. 3, c. 2; March 6, p. 3, c. 2; March 8, p. 3, c. 2; March 11, p. 3, c. 2; March 14, p. 3, c. 3; March 17, p. 3, c. 2.

[10]*Ibid.,* March 13, 1862, p. 3, c. 2; March 14, p. 2, c. 2; March 15, p. 3, c. 2.

themselves had not been designed for hospital use. Ingress and egress were badly arranged, and the prisoners on duty as nurses and orderlies found it fairly easy to make their escape. Iron bars were finally put into the rear windows of Hospital No. 3 as a preventive.[11]

Captain Ekin looked about for better quarters, and settled upon a frame building on the corner of Curve and Plum streets, east of the Bellefontaine car shops and north of Massachusetts Avenue. This could be fitted up for about eighty cots, and would allow the hospital in the Gymnasium to be dismantled. Patients and equipment were moved from Hospital No. 2 on April 3. Dr. Fletcher resigned at the time of the move and was succeeded by Dr. Livingston Dunlap, with Dr. J. H. Tilford as his assistant.[12]

Ever since Hoffman's visit, plans had been under way for the construction of an addition to the City Hospital, which would make a convenient and permanent provision for as many as three hundred sick prisoners. It would also be less expensive than several separate hospitals. Since the existing dispensary and kitchens could be used, the chief requirement would be additional nurses and attendants. It was thought that $2,500 would cover the cost of the addition.[13]

The main building was a three-story brick structure on the site of the present City Hospital. The addition erected to the north of the old building for the prisoners was of frame construction, a hundred feet long, forty-two feet wide, and three stories high.[14] It was completed in May, and by the twenty-fourth of that month the patients from the downtown hospital in the old post office and from the Bellefontaine hospital had been transferred there. The *Journal* describes it as follows:[15]

[11]*Ibid.*, March 14, 1862, p. 3, c. 2; April 1, p. 3, c. 1; Indianapolis *Sentinel*, March 13, 1862, p. 3, c. 2; March 22, p. 3, c. 2.

[12]Indianapolis *Journal*, March 25, 1862, p. 3, c. 1; April 3, p. 3, c. 2; April 4, p. 3, c. 2.

[13]*Official Records*, 2 series, III, 349, 375.

[14]*Ibid.*, III, 386-87; Indianapolis *Journal*, March 22, 1862, p. 3, c. 1.

[15]*Ibid.*, May 24, 1862, p. 3, c. 1-2. See also Indianapolis *Sentinel*, July 21, 1862, p. 3. c. 2.

"The stories are but nine feet, not quite so high as they should be, but as the building is only intended as a temporary summer hospital this defect is but slight. The wards are larger than those in the main building, and they are fully as comfortable, being well provided with windows, thus giving plenty of air and light. These wards are kept neat and clean, and no bad odor is emitted to nauseate both patients and attendants, as was the case with one of our down-town hospitals. . . . The number confined to a ward is greater than in the Federal hospital, but this is owing to the size of the rooms. None are crowded.

"The cooking is under the supervision of two Sisters of Providence, who employ only females for the purpose. Every article of food is well cooked and promptly furnished upon short notice. The two classes of patients of the convalescents [Union and Confederate] have separate dining rooms. . . . In fact the hospital is conducted in such a way that the two hospitals are almost as distinct as if they were miles apart. No intercourse whatever is allowed between our men and the prisoners. The arrangements for washing and ironing are complete. A constant change of clean clothes for the . . . patients and for their beds is supplied each week, or oftener, as occasion may require.

"The City Hospital has for over a year been under the charge of Dr. J. M. Kitchen, who has introduced such perfect system . . . that everything goes like clockwork. . . .

". . . In the prisoners' hospital, Dr. Wilkes, a Surgeon who was taken prisoner at Fort Donelson, is the Surgeon in charge. . . . The Hospital Steward, Dr. Reame, is one of the most industrious and faithful of men, and is a model of promptness and efficiency."

Enlargement of the receiving hospital at Camp Morton was also deemed advisable, and was carried out by putting in a second floor or half floor.[16] There was nothing elaborate about this institution. To save expense in furnishing, each patient was required to bring his own blanket. The steward, ward masters, nurses, cooks, and other assistants, all prisoners,

[16] *Official Records,* 2 series, III, 387, 401.

received no regular compensation, but Dr. Jameson gave them books and papers, and occasional small sums of money. According to his report of June 1, 1862, the whole number of patients admitted to the receiving hospital since March 11 was 700. Of these 127 were returned to quarters, 1 had died, 9 were still in the receiving hospital, and 563 had been sent to the emergency quarters in the city which have already been described.[17]

Many of the patients died, in spite of the best efforts of the surgeons. Exposure and poor fare for weeks before they reached Indianapolis left them too weak, too depressed, to make any effort at recovery. Although they found better quarters at Camp Morton than they had had for some time,[18] there was little about a prison camp to revive their spirits, and the cold weather of February and March had the worst possible effect. With the facilities of present-day hospitals at their disposal, they might have had some chance of recovery. but the military hospitals of 1862 were little more than shelters where the sick could be segregated from the well.

One physician described the pitiable condition of the Fort Donelson prisoners thus:[19] "The prevalent diseases among them were typhoid fever and typhoid pneumonia, occurring in persons in whom the vital forces had been reduced to the lowest possible degree; many 'dropped dead' while walking about their quarters, without having manifested any disease, organic or functional, except great general debility. In persons of this class, while moving about looking apparently in medium health, the action of the heart and arteries would be so feeble as to be scarcely perceptible in pulsations at the wrist."

Three Mississippians died on February 25, and the number of deaths increased rapidly. "The mortality among the prisoners does not abate," reported the *Journal* uneasily on March 24. "The list below shows thirty-two deaths last week, and 110 since the first arrival of prisoners here, being a greater

[17]Jameson, Report to Adjutant General Noble, June 1, 1862, Executive Department file, 109.9, 1861, Archives Division, Indiana State Library.

[18]Indianapolis *Journal,* March 8, 1862, p. 3, c. 2.

[19]*Medical and Surgical History of the War of the Rebellion,* Medical Volume, pt. III (Washington, 1888), 54.

number than have died at Chicago, where there are over 2,000 more prisoners." In April a case of smallpox appeared at Camp Morton. Dr. Jameson found it necessary to vaccinate about half the prisoners there, and fortunately this precaution prevented the spread of this most-dreaded disease.[20]

Although no epidemics swept through the camp or hospitals, it was not until June that the surgeons joined in reporting that general health conditions were much improved. The total number of deaths by the end of July was at least 265. In the humid month of August, Dr. Jameson was obliged to report an increase of dysentery and fevers at the camp. More than a hundred prisoners were too weak to be conveyed to Vicksburg late that month for exchange, but most of them were able to leave early in September. Eight hundred nineteen Confederates had by this time been treated in the City Hospital.[21]

Official medical records for these months are incomplete, although hospital stewards were instructed to transmit to Colonel Owen and Adjutant General Noble a report of all deaths, giving the name of the deceased, date of admittance to the hospital, company, regiment, and finally a list of any personal effects, which were to be held for delivery to relatives of the dead.[22] In the lists of deaths among the prisoners which appeared fairly regularly in the newspapers, the notation "name unknown" is not uncommon.[23]

By direction of Governor Morton, five lots were purchased near the City Cemetery for the interment of the Confederate prisoners who died at Camp Morton. The cemetery lay along Kentucky Avenue between West Street and the river, and came to be called by the name of one of its additions—Greenlawn. There was little ceremony about the burial services. Weaver and Williams, an Indianapolis firm of undertakers, had contracted to furnish plain wooden coffins for $3.50 each, and

[20]Indianapolis *Sentinel*, April 3, 1862, p. 3, c. 1.

[21]*Ibid.*, August 4, 1862, p. 3, c. 1; August 29, p. 3, c. 2; September 3, p. 3, c. 1; September 5, p. 3, c. 2.

[22]Noble, A. G. O., Letter and Order Book No. 1, pp. 195, 218; Indianapolis *Journal*, March 6, 1862, p. 3, c. 2.

[23]See especially weekly issues of Indianapolis *Sentinel*, March 4-July 24, 1862.

delivered the bodies at the cemetery. There details of prisoners dug the graves, trenches about twenty feet long in which the coffins were laid side by side, with a stout board carrying a painted identification number at the head of each one. If a burial service was read or a prayer offered, the rite was performed by one of the prisoners for his dead comrades.[24]

[24]Indianapolis *Journal*, February 27, 1862, p. 3, c. 2; March 18, p. 3, c. 2; Noble, A. G. O., Letter and Order Book No. 1, pp. 133, 134; Indianapolis *Sentinel*, February 26, 1862, p. 3, c. 2; March 6, p. 3, c. 2; January 31, 1865, p. 3, c. 1.

V. CAMP MORTON IN DECLINE, 1863

CAMP MORTON'S best period was past. By the beginning of 1863, the connection between camp and state administration was greatly lessened. Guards, supplies, inspections, camp improvements were under the control of the Federal Commissary General of Prisoners, and if everything was not always what the prisoners had a right to expect, state pride was not greatly affected. As far as the citizens and newspapers were concerned, prisoners had ceased to be an interesting novelty, and other concerns gradually thrust them from the public mind. Such circumstances as did recall them to notice—reports of the miseries suffered by Union prisoners in the South, or anti-administration attacks made more and more frequently on the purposes and conduct of the war—did them no service. From every point of view their fortunes changed for the worse with the prolongation of the war.

The prisoners' camp should have had a thorough renovation and rebuilding in the first months of 1863, for it was "much dilapidated and sadly in need of repairs."[1] For two years Union recruits and Confederate prisoners had crowded the barracks and swarmed over the enclosure. The buildings which dated from the camp's fairground days had been put to every use but the intended ones, and the few which had been erected since the beginning of the war were flimsy makeshifts designed on the theory that the war would soon be over. Nothing was ever done in anticipation of a probable need, and by the time the necessity of an improvement was acknowledged, weeks and months of delay had usually aggravated the need to twice its original proportions. From 1863 until 1865 the records contain a sorry round of inspectors' complaints and recommendations, and orders from the Commissary General of Prisoners in which permission for improvement was always balanced by the strictest exhortation to economy.

The capture of several thousand Confederates at the

[1] *Official Records*, 2 series, V, 227.

Arkansas Post and at Murfreesboro in January, 1863, found prison camp officials as unprepared as the first large captures made in 1862. Exchanges had been proceeding at City Point, Virginia, and at Vicksburg, but were now halted at the latter point by fighting in the area, and by the reluctance of the Union command to reinforce a city which they were intent on reducing.[2]

The prisoners were sent to St. Louis, where they were held for several miserable days on the boats until quarters could be found for them. To an inquiry about Camp Morton, Adjutant General Noble replied that the barracks could be made to accommodate two thousand prisoners, but no guard was available. The lack of a sufficient guard was particularly unfortunate at Indianapolis, where the number of secession sympathizers and anti-administration politicians was steadily growing, but Hoffman had no better station available, and the prisoners were divided between Camp Morton and Camp Douglas.[3]

Beginning on January 29, they reached Indianapolis in lots of from two to three hundred, until, by the end of March, 652 prisoners were lodged in the tumble-down barracks. Nearly all of them had been captured in the hospitals at Murfreesboro. They came from Kentucky, Tennessee, and Alabama regiments; perhaps a dozen of them had been at Camp Morton with the Fort Donelson prisoners. Among them were about ninety badly wounded, who were dispatched to the Central Hospital; 172 less seriously injured had to be taken care of in the old hospital at Camp Morton, and in one of the barracks which was taken over for their use.[4]

Because there was no crowding, the Murfreesboro prisoners fared reasonably well. The drafty sheds along the north side of the enclosure remained unoccupied. A fatigue party worked hard at policing the camp, and although no major repairs were made on the barracks, Captain Ekin furnished a

[2]*Official Records,* 2 series, V, 163, 176, 179-80.
[3]*Ibid.,* V, 201, 203-4, 228.
[4]*Ibid.,* V, 227-28, 391-92; Indianapolis *Journal,* January 29, 1863, p. 3, c. 3; February 12, p. 3, c. 1; Indianapolis *Sentinel,* January 30, 1863, p. 3, c. 1; February 16, p. 3, c. 1; March 2, p. 3, c. 1.

carpenter who constructed some bunks, and put in additional windows. It was recommended that several temporary barracks at Camp Carrington (one of the many Indianapolis camps for Union soldiers) be brought to Camp Morton in anticipation of a larger number of prisoners, but the move was not ordered. Five large buildings were in use, one 40 by 24 feet, one 110 by 20, two 100 by 20, and one 120 by 20 feet. Nurses and noncommissioned officers attached to the hospitals were quartered in three small buildings.[5]

Colonel James Biddle, of the Seventy-first Indiana Volunteers, commanded the camp. Most of his regiment, captured by Morgan at Muldraugh's Hill, Kentucky, on December 28, and paroled on the field, were now at Camp Morton awaiting exchange. The 250 men of the regiment not on parole were assigned to guard the prisoners, with two companies of the Sixty-third assisting them. Other administrative officers included Captain Ekin, of the quartermaster department, and his assistant, Captain L. L. Moore, who also had charge of the camp commissary. No issues of clothes were deemed necessary, for the prisoners had arrived warmly, if not uniformly clad, and most of them in possession of blankets. Supplies, furnished by Captain Thomas Foster, Jr., assistant commissary of subsistence, were rated as "good and wholesome in all parts," and the ration was mentioned as quite sufficient. Bread still came from the bakehouse managed by the state quartermaster general.

Assistant Surgeon A. N. Weir, of the Seventy-first Indiana, headed the medical department, with two Indianapolis physicians, Dr. David Funkhouser and Dr. Patrick H. Jameson, employed by contract as assistants. Funkhouser was the only one of these physicians who continued active at the camp during the summer. Although patients crowded the two hospital buildings, a camp inspector reported on March 24 that the cases were all old ones, principally wounded, and that under the circumstances the total of twenty-three deaths since the end of January was not alarming. No cases of smallpox had appeared.[6] His report seems unduly cheerful, for Dr. Funk-

[5]*Official Records,* 2 series, V, 227-28, 239-40, 391-92.
[6]*Ibid.,* V, 391-92.

houser announced in the Indianapolis *Sentinel* two days later that the wounded prisoners had been almost entirely without rags and bandages for some time, and entreated "humanely disposed" citizens of Indianapolis to contribute supplies.[7]

Whatever the lacks in camp and hospital equipment, the prisoners at Camp Morton at this period seemed to the inspector more cheerful and happy than at other posts. Besides being cleanly in appearance and performing the required police duties with willingness and alacrity, they showed a healthy zest for games and exercise that was uncommon in a prison camp.

Their imprisonment lasted less than three months. Exchange of enlisted men was still progressing, although indignation at the attitude of the Confederates toward commanders of negro troops had put an end to the exchange of officers.[8] The prisoners from Camp Morton were ordered to City Point, Virginia, and on April 6 and 23 almost six hundred began the long journey. Some of the wounded had to be taken to the station in wagons and ambulances, while many more hobbled along with the aid of canes; such a trip was a severe test of their fortitude and endurance.[9]

Authorities rejoiced to see them go. Ever since the draft of August, 1862, opposition to the administration and the war had come more and more into the open. In December, Colonel Henry B. Carrington felt impelled to report to the Secretary of War the spread in Indiana of a secret order which incited the desertion of soldiers with their arms, furthered resistance to arrest of deserters, and exerted its influence to stop enlistments and prevent the carrying out of the draft.[10]

In March, 1863, at Governor Morton's request, Carrington forwarded a memorandum on continued activities of the Knights of the Golden Circle:[11] in several counties arrest of deserters had met with armed resistance; nearly 30,000 arms had entered the state in February and March alone, and

[7]Indianapolis *Sentinel*, March 26, 1863, p. 3, c. 2.

[8]*Official Records*, 2 series, V, 192-93, 199, 234-35, 318, 706.

[9]*Ibid.*, V, 357; Indianapolis *Journal*, April 7, 1863, p. 3, c. 1; Indianapolis *Sentinel*, April 23, 1863, p. 3, c. 3.

[10]*Official Records*, 2 series, V, 108.

[11]*Ibid.*, V, 363-67. The names "Order of American Knights" and "Sons of Liberty" were used later.

plans had been discussed contemplating the seizure of the arsenal, railroads, and telegraph; kegs of powder were being smuggled in in boxes marked "nails" or "pickaxes." Carrington said that Indiana membership in the order had been put at 92,000 persons, and with lodges in all but seven counties, he was inclined to believe the number might not be extravagant.[12] Bitterness and recklessness were becoming more evident day by day. "I am convinced," said Carrington, "that the tension cannot long last; reaction or violence is certain."

It seemed to Morton, Carrington, and Brigadier General Orlando B. Willcox, commanding the military district of Indiana and Michigan, no time to introduce a large body of prisoners into the distraught community. Camp Morton was a big place, and at least six companies would be required to guard it efficiently. No one wanted to spare so many men for guard duty when there was every chance that disturbances in the state would require their services, or that General Morgan might suddenly appear north of the Ohio and start raiding operations in Indiana. Turning the camp over to prisoners also meant that some other place had to be found for assembling Indiana recruits or paroled troops.

Hoffman saw clearly enough that the camp system was inadequate and inconvenient, and suggested the building of one big depot capable of holding eight or ten thousand prisoners, but his estimate that the cost would run to $50,000 quashed any interest the War Department might have had in the idea.[13] The old camps had to serve.

The next group of prisoners to arrive at Camp Morton came from Gallatin, Tennessee, late in May. Grant's successful operations near Vicksburg provided a much larger installment within the week, when 4,400 Confederates were sent north to be divided between Camp Morton and Fort Delaware. Three trainloads came in on the afternoon of June 2, and once again the townspeople turned out to watch their entry. Ragged and travel-stained as they were, they had a hardy,

[12]Logan Esarey, in his *History of Indiana*, II, 781, says there "were perhaps 50,000 members" in 1863.

[13]*Official Records*, 2 series, V, 511-13.

vigorous appearance that was commented on by both the *Journal* and the *Sentinel*. On the next day, the remainder of the 4,400 arrived. Their officers, scheduled to go on to Camp Johnson, were fed and lodged for the night at the Soldiers' Home, which had been built the preceding summer to provide temporary shelter and refreshment for transient soldiers.[14]

A group of conscripted East Tennesseans among the prisoners attracted much attention. Their petition to take the oath of allegiance and enlist with the Union troops was warmly seconded by the *Journal,* which described them enthusiastically as "great stalwart men with frames like giants, bare-footed, bronzed with exposure, hardy as their own hills, as brave as men can be."[15] The War Department had frowned on the enlistment of prisoners of war, but the practice had continued sporadically at the camps, and Secretary Stanton was soon to give it his approval.[16] At Camp Morton, 250 Tennesseans took the oath of allegiance some time before June 12, and immediately enlisted—50 in the Seventy-first Indiana, 50 in the batteries, 155 in the Fifth Tennessee Cavalry. Quite a parade was made of the departure of this last group for Lexington on June 13. With an escort from the Seventy-first Indiana they marched down Pennsylvania Street to Market and through the heart of town to the Union Station where they entrained with rousing cheers for the Union.[17]

Willcox protested to Hoffman on June 11 that it was highly impolitic to keep the prisoners at Indianapolis, and asked where he could send them. Hoffman telegraphed permission to forward them to Fort Delaware, but it appears from the record that Willcox had started most of them to Camp Chase before Hoffman's message was received (there were only 111 prisoners in the camp on July 1). In a letter written

[14]Indianapolis *Sentinel,* May 30, 1863, p. 3, c. 1; June 3, p. 3, c. 3; June 4, p. 3, c. 3; June 8, p. 3, c. 1; June 12, p. 3, c. 1; Indianapolis *Journal,* June 1, 1863, p. 3, c. 1; June 3, p. 3, c. 3; June 4, p. 3, c. 2, 4; *Official Records,* 2 series, V, 722, 728.

[15]Indianapolis *Journal,* June 12, 1863, p. 2, c. 2-3.

[16]*Official Records,* 2 series, V, 242, 297, 345, 381-82, 446, 659, 669, 707; VI, 31, 186.

[17]Indianapolis *Journal,* June 12, 1863, p. 3, c. 1, 2; June 15, p. 3, c. 2, 3; Indianapolis *Sentinel,* June 12, 1863, p. 3, c. 1; June 15, p. 3, c. 2.

the same day, the Commissary General of Prisoners made it perfectly plain that Camp Morton could not be dispensed with, for the other camps were not much better able to hold the prisoners securely, and altogether would not accommodate more than twelve or fifteen thousand.[18] He pointed out that recent exchanges had released all of the Seventy-first (Biddle's regiment), the Fifty-first, and Sixty-third Indiana regiments, which could be assigned as guards.[19] Willcox acknowledged this letter with a reiterated warning that Camp Morton was no safe spot for prisoners.[20]

A week after Willcox had hustled off most of his prisoners, Captain Thomas H. Hines, of Morgan's Cavalry, crossed the Ohio into Perry County with less than a hundred men. For a soul-satisfying day, he proceeded calmly through the country toward Paoli in the guise of a Union officer in search of deserters. He actually arrested two. Whenever he saw a promising cavalry mount, he gathered it in, leaving the owner in happy possession of a broken-down horse and a generous voucher on the Federal quartermaster at Indianapolis. But the next day his secret was out, and Hines fell into the hands of a conscripted "guide" as impudent as himself. Under pretext of eluding the Legion companies which were springing to action on right and left, the guide led him to Blue River Island, with the assurance that it was a practicable fording point. It was, as far as the island, but on the southern side the current ran deep and strong. By the time the Confederates had made their devious and long-drawn-out march to the island, Indiana legionnaires were in position to block retreat. They opened fire, killing several Confederates and wounding several more. Hines made his escape by swimming the river, but fifty men and two officers were captured and dispatched to Louisville.[21] This incursion, brief and ineffective as it was, had no soothing effect on Indianapolis.

[18]*Official Records*, 2 series, V, 441; VI, 3; Indianapolis *Sentinel*, June 12, 1863, p. 3, c. 1; June 13, p. 3, c. 2.

[19]*Official Records*, 2 series, V, 400, 408, 409, 414, 584, 735.

[20]*Ibid.*, VI, 19-20.

[21]Terrell, *Report*, I, 161-65; Indianapolis *Journal*, June 23, 1863, p. 2, c. 1-2; Louis B. Ewbank, *Morgan's Raid in Indiana* (Indiana Historical Society *Publications*, VII, no. 2, Indianapolis), 135-39; Basil W. Duke, *History of Morgan's Cavalry* (Cincinnati, 1867), 430-31.

Two weeks later came the word that General John Morgan had started north through Kentucky. To help repel this invasion, practically all the United States troops in Indianapolis were ordered to Louisville, leaving the city thinly guarded by two companies of the Sixty-third Indiana, some hundreds of recently exchanged prisoners of the Fifty-first and Seventy-third regiments, and a few recruits. Into the general gloom trickled news of victories at Gettysburg and Vicksburg, and on July 7 the citizens celebrated with bonfires, fireworks, and speeches. Next day they heard that Morgan had crossed the Ohio at Brandenburg.[22]

Out from Governor Morton's office on Thursday, July 9, went a general order to all able-bodied men in the several counties south of the National Road to form themselves into companies of at least sixty persons, elect officers, and arm themselves as best they could. In Indianapolis alarm bells summoned the townspeople to listen to an order closing all places of business at three o'clock that afternoon, so that military companies might be formed in preparation for possible danger.

Reports credited Morgan with at least four thousand men and four pieces of artillery. Morton and Willcox both feared that he might move directly on the capital to release rebel prisoners, destroy the arsenal with all its arms and ammunition, and perhaps burn the city. The Governor asked for the return of the Seventy-first Indiana and Myer's Battery, which had been recently sent to Kentucky, and then hesitated to trust them to the railroad for fear they would be derailed or entrapped on route by the Confederates.

A city regiment was organized almost overnight, and drilled in University Square, while eight additional companies were forming in various wards. Banks had sent their specie northward for safety; business houses, except for the grocery

[22]For accounts of Morgan's raid, see Terrell, *Report*, I, 165-202, and Appendix, pp. 279-80; Duke, *History of Morgan's Cavalry*, 430-39; Basil W. Duke, Orlando B. Willcox, and Thomas H. Hines, "A Romance of Morgan's Rough Riders," in *Century*, XLI, 402-25 (January, 1891); Ewbank, *Morgan's Raid*, 140-83; Foulke, *Life of Morton*, I, 278-85; *Official Records*, 1 series, XXIII, pt. 1, 632 ff.; Holliday, *Indianapolis and the Civil War*, 582-83; Indianapolis *Journal*, July 15, 1863, p. 2, c. 2-4.

stores and newspapers, shut their doors. For three days armed men poured into the city. By Saturday the streets were crowded, camp fires burned in every grove, and Morton had to ask that no more men be sent. Occasionally the alarm bell rang, but Morgan did not come, and on the fourteenth it was established that he had moved out of Indiana into Ohio.

No miracle of restraint could have concealed from the prisoners the flurry and bustle in the near-by barracks. How soon they discovered that Morgan was on the march we have no way of knowing, but if, as Carrington suspected, they had contacts with secession sympathizers in the vicinity, they probably guessed why Colonel Biddle and his regiment were suddenly withdrawn, and why the camp was left in charge of Captain Albert J. Guthridge and a curtailed guard.

Their last hope of a dramatic rescue died on July 23, when eleven hundred of Morgan's men who had been captured in Ohio were brought to join them.[23]   A hundred more arrived a week later.[24]

No other prisoners ever confined at Camp Morton excited such interest as the men from Morgan's command. After their spectacular will-o'-the-wisp flight through the southern counties, it seemed almost incredible that they could be clapped into a prison camp like ordinary mortals. They were subjected to the thorough search which all prisoners had to undergo. This one proved unusually productive, for spoils of the raid began to appear in little wads of greenbacks—$20 extracted from one man's pipe bowl, $1,100 from another's canteen.[25]

After this initiation, the prisoners were allowed more than the usual latitude in receiving visitors. This was doubtless due to the slackening of camp discipline under temporary commandants. Guthridge, Biddle's immediate successor, had served only until July 23,[26] when he was relieved by Captain

[23]Indianapolis *Sentinel*, July 24, 1863, p. 3, c. 1; July 25, p. 3, c. 1; Indianapolis *Journal*, July 25, 1863, p. 2, c. 1, p. 3, c. 1, 2.

[24]*Ibid.*, July 30, 1863, p. 3, c. 3.

[25]*Ibid.*, July 27, 1863, p. 2, c. 1.

[26]Post Special Orders 15, Indianapolis, July 23, 1863, Newton D. Mereness Calendar of Papers from the National Archives (hereafter cited as Mereness Calendar), War Department, Northern Department Orders, Vol. 116, pp. 48-49.

David W. Hamilton, of the Seventh Indiana. Hamilton was a native of Kentucky, and many of Morgan's men came from wealthy and respected Kentucky families. Hardly had they reached Camp Morton, wrote an outraged and anonymous observer to Colonel Hoffman, "until their friends crowded to see them, furnishing them with money and clothing and various articles of food, treating and talking to them as martyrs and heroes. . . . I am informed," continued the writer, "that the permission to visit these rebels comes from General Burnside and General Willcox, and you can see at the Bates House ladies and gentlemen from Kentucky flourishing their permits and boasting of the prowess of their relatives in the Confederate Army."[27] There is evidence that some of the visitors were loyal Unionists, come to beg their sons to take the oath of allegiance. They had no success with Morgan's ardent young followers.[28]

Taking due notice of the questionable form in which these charges were made, Hoffman referred them to the Secretary of War, who sent dispatches to Burnside, Willcox, and Morton directing them to correct any undesirable laxness. Restrictions were put into effect at once,[29] greatly to the relief of Lieutenant Edward J. Robinson, newly appointed to act as commissary of prisoners at Camp Morton. He had reached the camp on July 8, to find "no rolls or books, and everything in confusion in all matters pertaining to prisoners of war and the camp in general." The appearance of the Morgan prisoners and their visitors had increased confusion to a point where Robinson found himself grudgingly "waiting on them all day" and compelled to work on the prison rolls at night.[30]

Inside the camp, the Morgan raiders proved equally disturbing. They made trouble among the other prisoners, and there were quarrels and riots that called for interference from the guards. A particular antipathy showed itself between this group and the Tennesseans, several hundred of whom

[27]*Official Records,* 2 series, VI, 162-63.
[28]Indianapolis *Journal,* July 27, 1863, p. 2, c. 1.
[29]*Ibid.,* July 29, 1863, p. 3, c. 3 ; August 15, p. 3, c. 2 ; Indianapolis *Sentinel,* August 6, 1863, p. 3, c. 1 ; *Official Records,* 2 series, VI, 257.
[30]*Ibid.,* VI, 195.

were proposing to take the oath of allegiance and enlist as Union soldiers.[31]

During the first two weeks of August eighteen hundred Confederates taken at the siege of Port Hudson, Louisiana, and in the campaign around Jackson, Tennessee, brought the total of prisoners at Camp Morton to about three thousand. According to the Indianapolis *Sentinel,* they were divided in the following proportions: from Tennessee, 830; Kentucky, 680; Arkansas, 631; Mississippi, 331; Alabama, 131; Louisiana, 106; Georgia, 106; Florida, 50; South Carolina, 51; North Carolina, 50. Over eleven hundred men, including most of Morgan's raiders, were transferred to Camp Douglas on August 17 and 18, and comparative quiet settled down on Camp Morton. About fifteen hundred prisoners remained in the squalid and unhealthy camp. Twenty-six men had died there during August, and ninety-eight were on the sick list.[32]

Inadequate hospital facilities had been worrying the medical officers all spring and summer. The addition to the City Hospital, built for prisoners from the prisoners' fund, had been gradually appropriated for Union wounded during the last quarter of 1862 and the first quarter of 1863, when there were very few Confederates at Camp Morton. When the problem of accommodating prisoner sick arose again with the arrival of prisoners from the Vicksburg campaign, there were two possible ways of meeting it: (1) the Union soldiers could be turned out of one wing of the City Hospital and the Confederates moved in, in which case a new hospital would have to be built to take care of the Federal overflow; (2) the Union soldiers could be left in possession of the City Hospital and new quarters provided for the rebels at Camp Morton.

Local officials inclined to the second plan, which would keep the two groups of hospital cases entirely separate and

[31]Indianapolis *Journal,* August 18, 1863, p. 3, c. 2; September 23, p. 3, c. 1; Post Special Orders, 34, 36, and 38, Indianapolis, August 19, 22, and 24, 1863, Mereness Calendar, War Department, Northern Department Orders, Vol. 116, pp. 59-61. One of the prisoners who took the oath and enlisted in the Seventh Cavalry came off winner in a buffalo chase held at the Fairgrounds in September.

[32]Indianapolis *Journal,* August 3, 1863, p. 3, c. 1; August 8, p. 3, c. 2, 3; August 15, p. 3, c. 2; Indianapolis *Sentinel,* August 19, 1863, p. 3, c. 2.

eliminate the necessity for extra guards outside the camp. If it had been promptly carried out, their choice would have seemed a sensible one, but they neglected to report the circumstances to the Commissary General of Prisoners, and the result was an agonizing delay. Meanwhile, the number of prisoners in camp doubled and trebled, and the need grew desperate.

Captain Ekin, of the quartermaster's department, telegraphed to Commissary General Meigs early in June that additional hospital space was "required" at Camp Morton, and suggested that a temporary addition to the old hospital building would meet the "emergency" economically. Four days later he telegraphed again that the situation was urgent.[33] There was no immediate response, but some weeks later a medical inspector, making the rounds of prison camps to report on the causes of sickness and mortality, stopped at Camp Morton.[34]

He found the hospital capacity limited to eighty-three old wooden bunks, some of them occupied by two patients. Bedding was scanty. Even air space was woefully limited—in some wards not more than 350 cubic feet per man, so that on a blistering summer day the quarters must have been stifling. A faulty diet, lacking in vegetables except for an occasional issue of potatoes, also operated against quick recoveries. Inspector Humphreys earnestly recommended increased accommodations, and Dr. Bobbs followed up with a request for permission to buy ice for the hospitals.[35]

Some of the illness was attributed by Humphreys to the poor drainage of the camp. The little ditch which the prisoners called "the Potomac" was flooded in the rainy seasons, while in hot dry weather it disappeared except for a few stagnant pools. In these the prisoners washed their clothes. Camp police was bad, sinks were filthy, and barracks were overcrowded. Finally, many of the prisoners disregarded all rules of cleanliness and were consequently "profusely verminous."

From this report, forwarded to him from the Surgeon

[33]*Official Records*, 2 series, V, 741, 762.
[34]Report of Lewis Humphreys, July 3, 1863, photostat in Indiana Division, Indiana State Library, from War Department, Northern Department Letter Books, Vol. 199, pp. 38-40.
[35]*Ibid.*, p. 38.

General's office, Colonel Hoffman apparently received his first intimation that the new wing of the City Hospital was no longer at the disposal of Confederate prisoners. On July 16, 1863, he wrote to General Willcox asking for information, and expressing his desire that the building be used for the purpose for which it had been erected. Willcox thereupon ordered Bobbs to remove part of the Federal sick from the City Hospital and release one wing for prisoners.[36]

Dr. Bobbs was in a most uncomfortable position. He knew the storm that such a move would provoke, for many citizens were already passionately indignant at the hardships Union prisoners had suffered at Libby and Belle Isle prisons in Richmond, and some had gone so far as to advocate retaliation. Bobbs hastily filed his objections with the Medical Director of the Department of the Ohio, pointing out the practical difficulties involved in carrying out the order, and the certainty of resentment and exasperation among the people of Indiana. At the same time he emphasized the immediate need for enlargement of the hospital at Camp Morton. The result was the suspension of Willcox's order, and instructions to place the Confederate sick in tents if necessary.[37] Bobbs could only hope that a new appeal through the quartermaster's department would be more effective. In the meantime some tents were put into service for hospital cases.[38]

After reading the official reports referred to above, it is difficult to explain an item which appeared in the Indianapolis *Sentinel* of August 28, quoting Dr. Funkhouser to the effect that hospital arrangements at Camp Morton were admirable, and that everything necessary was done for the comfort of sick rebel prisoners in the city.[39] It is probable that camp

[36]*Official Records,* 2 series, VI, 122-23; Bobbs to W. H. Church, Medical Director, Department of the Ohio, July 26, 1863, photostat, in Indiana Division, Indiana State Library, from War Department, Northern Department Letter Books, Vol. 199, pp. 51-53.

[37]Bobbs to Church, *op. cit.*

[38]Bobbs to Ekin, July 24, 1863, and Ekin to Meigs, same date, Mereness Calendar, War Department, Quartermaster General, Letters Received; Bobbs to J. T. Carpenter, Cincinnati, Ohio, September 10, 1863, *ibid.*, War Department, Northern Department Letter Books, Vol. 199, pp. 91-92.

[39]Indianapolis *Sentinel,* August 28, 1863, p. 3, c. 1.

officials were guarding against any public outcry on behalf of the prisoners that might provide fuel for secession sympathizers. A similar item, appearing a few days later and commenting on the issue of blankets to the prisoners during the recent cool weather, ended with a distinct note of self-satisfaction: "We certainly, here in Indiana, will treat our prisoners of war as men unfortunately in our hands, and we ardently hope that brave and gallant Hoosiers in limbo in the South will be likewise looked after."[40]

Actually conditions grew steadily worse, and there was no hope for improvement as long as command of the camp continued to be transferred at short intervals. Hamilton, who had taken charge on July 23, was transferred elsewhere sometime before September 23, and Captain Guthridge was recalled for a second brief term as stop-gap commandant.[41]

The guards at Camp Morton during this period were the Fifty-first and Seventy-third Indiana regiments, whose officers were still held prisoners at Richmond. Several months on parole, and the lack of any commissioned officers except seven who had been recently appointed, had left them badly demoralized and undisciplined.[42] Quick to take advantage of a slack guard, numbers of prisoners started laying plans for escape. One group, after working for twelve days on a tunnel under the north fence of the enclosure, was betrayed on the eve of escape; several other groups were caught after they had got outside the enclosure; but thirty-five men got safely away between the first of August and the end of October.[43]

In September, Medical Inspector Humphreys visited Camp Morton again, and added to his earlier complaints other distressing comments: there were dead animals near the camp; the post-mortem rooms and dead house were not in good

[40]*Ibid.,* August 31, 1863, p. 3, c. 1.

[41]The date of the transfer has not been found. Hamilton was still in command on August 25 (Indianapolis *Journal,* August 25, 1863, p. 3, c. 2), and Guthridge had succeeded him by September 23 (*ibid.,* September 23, 1863, p. 3, c. 1).

[42]*Official Records,* 2 series, VI, 143-44, 492-93.

[43]*Post,* p. 379; Indianapolis *Journal,* September 23, 1863, p. 3, c. 1; Indianapolis *Sentinel,* September 24, 1863, p. 3, c. 2.

condition; the largest barracks was unfit for winter use.[44] But this was mild in comparison with the scorching report made on October 22 by Augustus M. Clark, another medical inspector. It is quoted in full because it covers the physical condition of the camp with such thoroughness, and shows the difficult situation faced by the commandant who took office on that date:[45]

"Designation of camp—Camp Morton. Commander of camp—Captain Guthridge, Forty-eighth Indiana Volunteers, this day relieved by Colonel Stevens, Invalid Corps. Command and strength—prisoners, rebel officers, 7; rebel soldiers, 2,325; civilians, 30; total, 2,362. Location of camp—one mile and a half north of Indianapolis, Ind. Time occupied—about eighteen months. Water, source and supply—by pumps from wells, five in number; supply, sufficient. Water, quality and effects—good, slightly alkaline. Fuel—wood and coal. Soil—clay and sand, muddy. Drainage—bad from want of attention; ditches and drains choked with rubbish. Topography—ground level, some trees, deep ditch, formerly bed of a creek running through middle of camp. Police of camp—very bad. Discipline in camp—lax. Tents or huts, position—barracks on north and west sides of square. Tents or huts, pattern and quality—one story and in dilapidated condition. Tents or huts, ventilation—only ventilated from dilapidation. Tents or huts, sufficiency—the barracks at present used for prison purposes are sufficient for 2,000 to 2,200 prisoners. Tents or huts, heating—stoves in a few of the barracks. Sinks, construction—exceedingly faulty, two excavations about twenty feet long, five feet wide, two feet deep, entirely open. Sinks, condition and position—very foul, one on north side about 25 feet in rear of barracks; on west side about 100 feet in rear. Sinks, management—no management at all. Removal of offal, &c.—unattended to; the central ditch is a general receptacle for refuse of all kinds. Previous use of camp—State fair-ground. Rations—abundant and of good quality. Cooking in camp—by prisoners over camp-fires. Inspection

[44]Quoted in John M. Cuyler to the Surgeon General, October 13, 1863, photostat in Indiana Division, Indiana State Library, from War Department, Northern Department Letter Books, Vol. 199, pp. 118-19.

[45]*Official Records,* 2 series, VI, 424-26.

of food—said to be inspected by commanding officer. Portable ovens—none, bread furnished by commissary. Vegetables— potatoes only.

"Cleanliness of men and clothing—foul; bathing and laundry facilities entirely insufficient. Quality and quantity of clothing obtained from quartermaster's department—sufficient. Blankets and bedding—insufficient both in hospital and camp; no satisfactory reason given therefor. Condition of men—in barracks, exceedingly foul; in hospital, miserable. Hospital buildings—two, one dilapidated and utterly unfit for use; the other (former guard-house) in good condition, but much overcrowded. Hospital tents—six, destitute of stoves or other means of heating. Hospital police—very much neglected, especially in cook-house, which is in filthy condition. Hospital discipline—none to speak of. Hospital diet and cooking—very little if any attention paid by officers. Hospital heat and ventilation—heated sufficiently by stoves except in tents; the guard-house ward is properly ventilated, the other only by dilapidation. Hospital capacity—36 in tents, 12 in guard-house ward; total, 48. Number sick—216; of these 125 are in barracks who should be in hospital and well taken care of. State of medical supplies—sufficient, but very disorderly kept. State of surgical instruments—none in hospital. State of hospital records—carelessly kept. State of hospital fund— $368, September 30, 1863. Reports—carelessly made. Medical attendance—virtually none. Nursing—by prisoners. Interments—by contract. Diseases, local—pulmonic, diarrhea, several cases of scurvy. Diseases, prevention of—no care taken. Recoveries from diseases—slow and uncertain. Mortality from diseases—during the month of September 23 out of 183 patients died, being over 12.45 per cent. Medical officer—Acting Assistant Surgeon Funkhauser. This officer is utterly unfit for the post he holds. I am informed that his contract is for $100 per month. This requires him to devote his whole time to his hospital and camp duties to the exclusion of all outside business. I am also informed that he has a large outside practice, and that he usually (and sometimes omitting even this) visits the camp not to exceed half an hour daily, leaving the almost entire charge of the sick and everything pertaining to the sanitary management of the camp to an enlisted man, who, though he has paid some attention to the study of medicine, and endeavors to do his best, is entirely unequal to the proper discharge of these duties. As a consequence of this the sick are neglected or improperly treated; the ratio of mortality is unwarrantably large, the hospital is in a most lamentable condition, and the general sanitary management of the camp is utterly neglected. I would respectfully suggest that this officer be at once removed and a competent man assigned in his stead.

"As the foregoing report will show, this camp is a disgrace to the name of military prison. It is filthy in every respect. The vicinity of the sinks is obvious for many yards around, they being perfectly open; no attempt made to disinfect them. They are, moreover, insufficient in number. The seven rebel officers confined here are crowded into a small room about ten by twelve and eight feet high. In this they sleep, live, and cook. There are good natural facilities for drainage, but the drains are choked with rubbish, and the large central ditch is a grand receptacle for the refuse of the whole camp. The main hospital ward is in so dilapidated a condition that the patients are obliged to fasten their blankets along the wall for partial protection from wind and weather, and are thus deprived of the necessary covering. In fact, every patient whom I examined had more or less of pulmonary trouble accompanying his disease, whatever it might be. The hospital cookhouse was in filthy condition, and the food which had just been prepared for dinner at the time of my visit was most miserably cooked. I found the bath and wash house used for storing straw for bedding. The hospital fund is not expended with sufficient freedom in procuring comforts for the sick, nor could I ascertain that any account of the less perishable articles, as table furniture, &c., purchased from the fund is kept. The commanding officer states that he has been directed to erect two additional hospital barracks, but they are not as yet commenced. The prison fund on hand September 30, 1863, was

$959.68. This fund is drawn on for repairs, cooking, police, utensils, &c., of which an account is kept.

A. M. CLARK,
Surgeon
and Acting Medical Inspector of Prisoners of War."

On the strength of this report, Hoffman refused to allow Funkhouser's account for services, and wrote to the Surgeon General asking that "a competent surgeon with an assistant . . . be ordered for duty at the camp without delay."[46] Funkhouser defended himself against Clark's charges, asserting that he had visited all patients at least once every day, and usually twice, in addition to looking after the men of the Fifth Regiment, Invalid Corps, recently quartered at Camp Burnside. "It is no fault of mine," he said bitterly, "that the Hospital Buildings have been exceedingly defective consisting of several old rickety sheds, a few Hospital tents together with some Wall and Bell Tents and Boards put together according to no well established Style of architecture, which doubtless have prejudiced in some degree the mind of Med. Inspector Clark. Better buildings you are aware were ordered, sometime ago, but for good reasons doubtless their construction has been delayed." Bobbs supported him, and asked for further consideration of the case, but Funkhouser was replaced by Dr. W. A. Johnson.[47]

The "better buildings" which Funkhouser mentioned, were two new hospital wards, which were not opened until December, 1863, and were not even then complete. They were designed to increase the hospital capacity to 160, allowing 800 cubic feet of air to each patient, and could be made to accommodate more than that number in emergencies. These wards were built by the quartermaster's department; to pay for

[46]*Official Records,* 2 series, VI, 442-43.

[47]Funkhouser to Bobbs, November 14, 1863, and Bobbs to Ekin, November 20, photostat in Indiana Division, Indiana State Library, from War Department, Northern Department Letter Books, Vol. 199, pp. 137-40; Bobbs to R. C. Wood, Louisville, Kentucky, February 27, and March 4, 1864, Mereness Calendar, War Department, Northern Department Letter Books, Vol. 199, pp. 325, 345; *Official Records,* 2 series, VI, 879.

them, an exchange for the prisoners' wing of the City Hospital was suggested, and may have been made.[48]

[48]Indianapolis *Sentinel,* November 2, 1863, p. 3, c. 2; Ekin to Quartermaster General Meigs, October 31, 1863, Mereness Calendar, War Department, Quartermaster General, Letters Received; *Official Records,* 2 series, VI, 879, 880; Carnahan, *Camp Morton,* 21-22.

VI. REORGANIZATION UNDER COLONEL STEVENS, 1863-64

COLONEL Ambrose A. Stevens, the new commandant, was regarded as a capable and intelligent officer. He had served as lieutenant colonel and colonel with the Michigan troops, was wounded at Perrysville, Kentucky, in October, 1862, and resigned the next February. When the Invalid Corps, later the Veteran Reserve Corps,[1] was created, Stevens received an appointment as major of the Fifth Regiment. This regiment was ordered to Indianapolis early in September, 1863, to relieve the Indiana troops on guard at Camp Morton. On September 25, Stevens was advanced to a colonelcy, and on October 22, was placed in command of Camp Morton.[2]

Stevens held this position until the end of the war, and was accounted an admirable commandant by the authorities, who were chiefly interested in preventing disturbances at the camp. His talents were not sufficiently diverse to make him entirely successful: although he was well-intentioned, he lacked discernment and intuition in dealing with the prisoners, and he was not impelled by the zeal on their behalf which made Owen unique among camp commandants.[3]

[1]Thomas Sturgis, in *Prisoners of War, 1861-65* (G. P. Putnam's Sons, 1912) 268-69, gives an amusing explanation of the change of name. The Invalid Corps was recruited for guard and garrison duty from men who were incapacitated for active service by wounds or disease. They wore on their light blue uniforms the insignia I. C., also used by the quartermaster's department to designate property which had been "inspected and condemned." The rebels soon learned the double significance of the lettering and joyously christened the Invalid Corps the "Condemned Yanks." To rescue its gallant veterans from this unholy ridicule, the Government renamed the Corps Veteran Reserves.

[2]Francis B. Heitman, *Historical Register . . . of the United States Army . . .*, I (Washington, D. C., 1903), p. 922; Indianapolis *Journal*, September 11, 1863, p. 3, c. 1; October 27, p. 3, c. 1. The Fifty-first and Seventy-third Indiana regiments, which had been guarding prisoners, left for Tennessee on October 23. *Ibid.*, October 26, 1863, p. 3, c. 1.

[3]Terrell, *Report*, I, Appendix, p. 285; Indianapolis *Sentinel*, July 30, 1864, p. 3, c. 1; *Official Records*, 2 series, VII, 71; Carnahan, *Camp Morton*, 19.

His first report indicates his limitations. Hoffman had sent him a copy of the rules governing prisoners' camps, and asked for a full report on conditions at Camp Morton. Stevens' reply was made on November 9, after a little more than two weeks in his new post.[4] It is a short, colorless document, substantiating without comment or amplification the criticisms made by Inspector Clark.[5]

Stevens devoted more than half his letter to the shortcomings of the old guard and his plans for the new one. As a preventive against further escapes, the daily patrols had been increased from 141 to 160 men, and again to 200, a number that he thought might be reduced if the guards had revolvers in addition to their muskets.[6] The unfitness of the barracks for winter occupancy and the insufficiency of the hospitals were disposed of in two sentences, and the proposed remedies in two more: "New and commodious hospitals are at present being erected for the accommodation of the sick. Repairing of the barracks had been commenced by Captain Guthridge, former commandant, which are now being continued, and when completed will be capable of accommodating 3,000 prisoners."

Stevens might have expatiated a little on these matters, for the "commodious" new hospitals were designed to care for only 160 cases while the sick list was over two hundred, and already the number of prisoners in camp was nearing or had passed the three thousand mark. He might have mentioned also that repairs to the barracks did not go beyond the squeezing in of extra bunks and a coat of whitewash. They remained unfloored, badly heated, and badly ventilated.

Reaching the subject of the prisoners, Stevens contented himself with remarking: "I found the prisoners generally supplied with necessaries, though in a poor state of health. The cause I am unable to determine, as our own troops quartered near them and equally crowded enjoyed excellent health."

[4]*Official Records,* 2 series, VI, 445-46.

[5]*Ibid.,* VI, 492-93.

[6]On November 27, 1863, Hoffman recommended to Stanton that 400 revolvers and 25,000 rounds of ammunition be sent to each prison camp. Camp Morton received its share early in December. *Official Records,* 2 series, VI, 584, 650.

Unfortunately for the prisoners then at Camp Morton and in all the other stations north and south, the Union and Confederate governments had reached an impasse on the subject of exchanges.[7] While the agents of the two governments quarreled over terms of parole, equivalents, and the status of negro soldiers, the despondent prisoners watched their hopes of early release dwindle and disappear. Public indignation at the interruption of exchange was fed by the efforts of each government to fasten the blame on the other. In the North, ugly stories about the southern prisons were given much prominence, and Secretary Stanton began to threaten retaliation. On November 9, 1863, he wrote to Major General Ethan A. Hitchcock, Union commissioner for exchange:[8] "You will please report what measures you have taken to ascertain the treatment of United States prisoners by the rebels at Richmond, and you are directed to take measures for precisely similar treatment toward all the prisoners held by the United States, in respect to food, clothing, medical treatment, and other necessaries."

Hitchcock replied that if treatment of Union prisoners at Richmond was what rumor represented, retaliation "would result in an uprising of the prisoners against their guards at Camps Morton and Chase," and probably at other places where the means of security were slender.[9] General Halleck deplored the adoption of a retaliatory policy on the more lofty ground that resort to "this extreme right," though fully justified by the laws and usages of war, was revolting to the sense of humanity.[10]

What followed was a series of everchanging regulations, based one moment on the theory that what was good enough for a Union prisoner was good enough for a Confederate, and the next on the theory that the Federal Government must uphold a standard of generous treatment to prisoners of war. It was difficult for the North to defend the imposition of unnecessary hardships on prisoners, in view of its relatively ample resources of money and food. The medical inspectors

[7]Hesseltine, *Civil War Prisons,* 99-113.
[8]*Official Records,* 2 series, VI, 485.
[9]*Ibid.,* VI, 486.
[10]*Ibid.,* VI, 523-24.

had no sympathy with such a policy, and the public, though it might clamor for retaliation, abhorred it in practice. As a result of this uncertain course, camp commanders had to be ready to alter their rules at a moment's notice: they must take respectful account of restrictive orders about food and clothing, but they must also avoid stirring up any hornets' nests by allowing reports to go out that prisoners were underfed or half frozen. The commandant who failed to preserve his balance on this tightrope was liable to a sharp reprimand.

At Camp Morton chilly weather had set in early, its first blasts foretelling a winter of extreme cold and heavy snows. The shivering Confederates found no comfort now in the open spaces that were Camp Morton's greatest asset in spring and summer, and none in the barracks, crowded toward the end of October by hundreds of additional prisoners from the Chattanooga area.[11] They packed the wooden sheds and overflowed into tents.

The new arrivals looked shabby and forlorn. Tattered remnants of the clothes in which they had begun the summer campaign scarcely covered their thin bodies. Many had no shoes. Wounds, exhaustion, and hunger brought them to Indianapolis "as nearly dead as alive," defenseless against the unaccustomed cold, and prime subjects for pneumonia, bronchitis, and typho-malarial fevers. In November the list of sick climbed to 328, and deaths totaled 68.[12]

Hoffman had requested Commissary General Meigs to reserve fifteen thousand suits of inferior clothing, the same quantity of blankets, and a larger number of shirts for the use of prisoners during the winter, but these had to be doled out sparingly because nobody knew how many prisoners might be added to the twelve or fifteen thousand already in the western camps.[13] The garments furnished by the Government

[11]Chattanooga prisoners continued to arrive until the last week in November. Indianapolis *Sentinel,* October 17, 1863, p. 3, c. 1; November 2, p. 3, c. 1; November 6, p. 3, c. 1; November 21, p. 3, c. 1; Indianapolis *Journal,* October 19, 1863, p. 3, c. 2; October 21, p. 3, c. 1; November 11, p. 3, c. 2; November 12, p. 3, c. 1; November 20, p. 3, c. 3.

[12]Carnahan, *Camp Morton,* 24, quoting J. W. Hosman, hospital steward from 1863 to 1865. *Post,* p. 379.

[13]*Official Records,* 2 series, VI, 468.

COLONEL AMBROSE A. STEVENS
Commandant, Camp Morton, 1863-65

were of regulation blue; to make sure that they were not used as a disguise by escaping Johnny Rebs, the coats were shorn of their buttons and long skirts, and incidentally made less effective protection against the cold. The prisoners hated the bobtailed Federal uniforms.[14]

At Camp Morton blankets and clothing were issued to the most destitute cases only. Stevens had reason to think that a small distribution was all that would be approved, for Hoffman wrote on November 12: "For the present you will issue no clothing of any kind except in cases of utmost necessity. So long as a prisoner has clothing upon him, however much torn, you must issue nothing to him, nor must you allow him to receive clothing from any but members of his immediate family, and only when they are in absolute want."[15]

The order was applied too literally to meet general approval, however. Captain Ekin, of the quartermaster's department, who had been in charge of erecting the two new hospital wards, thought that the patients were insufficiently clad, and without notifying Stevens, telegraphed Hoffman that they needed drawers, socks, and shirts. Hoffman promptly turned on Stevens, writing on December 17:[16] "This state of things should not exist, nor is it proper that the information should come to me through Captain Ekin. . . . there is no good [reason] why at any time there should be any deficiency of necessary articles."

Prisoners were still receiving sufficient rations in November, although lack of fresh vegetables induced some scurvy. The daily issue was three quarters of a pound of bacon or a pound of fresh beef, good wheat bread, hominy, coffee, tea, sugar, vinegar, candles, soap, salt, pepper, potatoes, and molasses. The food was of good quality, but each man cooked for himself, or with a small group of friends, and in this

[14]*Ibid.*, VI, 503-4.

[15]*Ibid.;* Indianapolis *Sentinel,* November 2, 1863, p. 3, c. 2. Clothing supplied by the prisoners' families was required to be gray in color. *Official Records,* 2 series, VI, 257.

[16]*Ibid.*, VI, 713. See also Hoffman's letter of February 19, 1864, to Brigadier General H. D. Terry, commanding at Sandusky, Ohio. *Ibid.*, VI, 972.

haphazard preparation wasted food and fuel, and ruined his digestive system. Hoffman undertook to reduce the losses by installing huge kettles called "Farmers' boilers," in which from 30 to 120 gallons of soup or stew could be prepared at once, but as usual the reform was accomplished slowly.[17]

The prisoner who had credit at the commandant's office could vary his diet with purchases from the camp sutler. He was also allowed to receive boxes of food from friends and relatives. On the first of December, 1863, both these privileges were suddenly cut off by Stanton's order—no more milk, butter, eggs, or canned fruit; worst of all, no more tobacco. The deprivation of tobacco caused more discontent than the short allowance of clothing, and Hoffman recommended that it be supplied from the prison fund rather than risk disturbances. Altogether, this experiment in retaliation was proving more awkward than anyone had anticipated. Sutlers had supplied postage stamps, letter paper, some underclothing, and other articles that were constantly in demand. Were these to be cut off too?[18]

During November and December the Confederate Government allowed quantities of blankets and provisions to be delivered by the Federal and state governments to Union prisoners in the South. It was also reported that the personnel of the southern prison commissariat had been changed for the better. By the end of December Stanton was convinced that the condition of Federal prisoners had been materially improved, and sent word to Hoffman to make up a list of articles which Confederate prisoners might purchase. Sale of tobacco, pipes, writing materials, and stamps was thereafter permitted, but for two freezing months when extra food would have been painfully welcome to the prisoners, none was allowed them.[19]

The turn of the year was stormy and fearfully cold. At one o'clock on the afternoon of Thursday, December 31, the temperature in Indianapolis stood at 40°—raw and chilling, but not severe to men accustomed to exposure. During the

[17]*Official Records,* 2 series, VI, 660-61, 702, 878.
[18]*Ibid.,* VI, 625, 628-29, 649-50, 701-2.
[19]*Ibid.,* VI, 774, 948, 967.

afternoon the mercury began a relentless descent; at eleven o'clock it passed the zero mark, and before sunrise on New Year's Day had reached 20° below. The cold wave extended far to the west and north, and south to Nashville, Tennessee. It closed over the Mississippi, freezing it clear across, "solid," the newspapers said, so that for several days heavy teams were able to cross on the ice.[20]

With the cold came a furious swirling snowstorm that half buried the town, blocking streets and stopping railroad transportation north and south. There was no comfort anywhere. New Year's Eve gatherings at the most luxurious homes in town were afterwards remembered less for their warmth and gaiety than because the guests barely escaped freezing on the way home. But this discomfort could be laughed at next day. At the other end of town, misery was not a matter of an hour. It fastened upon Camp Morton a grip that did not loosen for weeks.

Dismayed officials hurried about, making what provision they could for prisoners and guards. Raids on the city wood yards yielded a double ration of four-foot sticks for the cast-iron stoves in the barracks, and huge campfires were built in the enclosure. Extra straw was distributed too, but not enough to stop the sweep of wind and snow through cracks in the walls. (The total quantity of straw issued in December was 24,376 pounds—with 3,372 prisoners, each man's share was about 8 pounds.)[21] Finally, division by division, the prisoners were marched past headquarters, where seven hundred blankets and many pairs of shoes were given out.[22] Colonel Stevens had let regulations go by the board in his efforts to secure

[20]Indianapolis *Sentinel,* January 1, 1864, p. 3, c. 2, 5; January 4, p. 3, c. 1; Indianapolis *Journal,* January 1, 1864, p. 3, c. 4; January 2, p. 3, c. 1; January 4, p. 3, c. 1 .

[21]Carnahan, *Camp Morton,* 26, 28. The issues of wood and straw for the winter months are given as follows:

November, 1863, wood 542 cords; straw, 16,000 pounds
December, 1863, wood, 675 cords; straw, 24,376 pounds
January, 1864, wood, 600 cords; straw, 12,988 pounds
February, 1864, wood, 560 cords; straw, 8,818 pounds.

[22]"Treatment of Prisoners at Camp Morton," in *Century Magazine,* XLII, 761, 762.

extra clothing. On January 2, on the principle that confession of sin should follow as soon as possible on its commission, he sent off to Washington duplicate requisitions and an account of the emergency.[23]

In spite of these efforts at relief, suffering was intense. On the long shelves that served as bunks, the prisoners lay huddled together, usually in groups of three, with one man's blanket and a little straw beneath them, and the other two blankets, or more, if they were lucky, spread above. It was customary to take turns occupying the middle space, but occasionally someone was allowed to keep it permanently as a concession to extreme youth or frailty. The men slept spoon fashion—it made a shorter line and the blankets lay a little thicker—and at intervals through the unhappy night, a shivering end man would order his file to "Spoon!", a command that was answered by a mighty flop, as precisely executed as any maneuver on the parade ground.[24] None of the expedients so painfully learned during the first weeks of winter proved efficacious on the last night of 1863. The cold struck in to the men's very bones.

Outside, the guards were kept at their patrols, although there was little likelihood that any prisoners would be foolhardy enough to make a break on such a night. Officers took their watches with the men. They were ordered off the exposed sentinels' walk along the outside of the fence to make their rounds inside the enclosure, and they were relieved every hour, or oftener on call. The cry "Officer of the Gua-a-a-rd, Post Number 5," usually meant that a sentry's feet or hands were frosted. A number of them went to the hospital next day, and some suffered lasting injuries.[25] At the other camps in town, officers called in the sentinels, trusting the bitterness of the night to keep off marauders and camp followers.

[23]*Official Records,* 2 series, VI, 809.

[24]Wyeth, "Cold Cheer at Camp Morton," in *Century Magazine,* XLI, 846-47.

[25]Indianapolis *Sentinel,* January 4, 1864; Indianapolis *Journal,* January 2, 1864, p. 3, c. 1; January 4, p. 3, c. 1; January 5, p. 3, c. 2; Carnahan, *Camp Morton,* 27; "Treatment of Prisoners at Camp Morton," in *Century Magazine,* XLII, 761.

Under the stimulation of such extraordinary weather, rumor outran the distressing actuality: from ten to fifteen prisoners were said to have frozen to death on New Year's Eve; a guard had succumbed from exposure after being tied to a tree to keep him at his post; soldiers had frozen to death on stalled railroad trains.[26] Such stories were dangerous, and the Governor ordered General Carrington to investigate conditions in every camp in town. His report was calculated to quiet all outcry: there had been no deaths or serious injury among the guards; there was less sickness among the prisoners than usual; and they lacked nothing indispensable to their health and comfort. The men were described as "cheerful and thankful," and one was quoted as saying that it would be extravagant to ask for anything more than they had.[27]

Against this optimistic statement, we have the official prisoners' rolls, recording 91 deaths and 244 sick at Camp Morton in December, 1863, and 104 deaths and 251 sick in January, 1864. These figures include only the hospital cases. An inspection made on January 26 put the number of sick in hospital at 240, in barracks, at 706, making a total of 946. Nine men died in one day. Although camp officials then and afterwards denied vehemently that any prisoner ever froze to death at Camp Morton, the record carries an unavoidable implication that the abnormally cold weather, together with the shortage of warm clothing and blankets, brought on or hastened many deaths.[28]

Relief from the cold was slow in coming. Top temperature on New Year's Day was 12° below zero. The next afternoon it crept above zero, and on Sunday it reached 17° above, but there was snow all that night. On the fifth and sixth there was below-zero weather again. For the rest of the month cold blustery days predominated. February brought little relief.

[26]Indianapolis *Sentinel*, January 4, 1864, p. 3, c. 1, 2; Indianapolis *Journal*, January 4, p. 3, c. 1, 2; January 7, p. 2, c. 6.

[27]Indianapolis *Sentinel*, January 7, 1864, p. 3, c. 2; Indianapolis *Journal*, January 7, 1864, p. 2, c. 6.

[28]*Post*, p. 379; Wyeth, "Cold Cheer at Camp Morton," in *Century Magazine*, XLI, 847; "Treatment of Prisoners at Camp Morton," in *Century Magazine*, XLII, 761-62; Carnahan, *Camp Morton*, 31; *Official Records*, 2 series, VI, 878-79.

On the seventh a violent storm of rain, hail, and wind swept over Indianapolis. A week later came another period of bitter cold, followed by snow, rain, and more snow. On the fourth of March a "furious and universal" snowstorm raged. Spring lagged, farmers unable to plough or plant. The last snow to be recorded in the newspapers that season did not fall until April 16.[29]

Difficult as the situation was, Colonel Stevens succeeded in making enough improvements at the camp to draw a favorable comment from Inspector Clark when he visited Indianapolis toward the end of January.[30] Slackness in the guard had completely disappeared. Thanks to efficient policing, the enclosure was sloughing off its unkempt air, and one of the former eyesores, the trash-filled creek bed, had been transformed into a valuable addition to the drainage system.

Camp hospitals also showed a change for the better. Their capacity, including the two new wards and ten additional hospital tents, had been increased to 292, and the patients were now clean, comfortable, and better supplied with medical supplies and surgical instruments. Clark directed the purchase of three hundred outfits of clothing to be held for hospital use, and urged the enlargement of the kitchen and the construction of a hospital laundry to round out facilities. He was pleased with the staff. Dr. Johnson was a skillful and energetic officer, and responsible for many of the improvements. He had as assistants three acting assistant surgeons and two physicians from among the prisoners. Unfortunately, Johnson was determined to retire from service; in spite of Clark's attempt to dissuade him, he left Camp Morton in February and was succeeded by Surgeon Charles J. Kipp.

At the time of Clark's visit, patients with contagious diseases—measles was the commonest—were segregated in special hospital tents. In February three cases of smallpox appeared, possibly brought into camp by a small body of prisoners who arrived on February 14. Stevens wrote for permission to establish a tent hospital outside the enclosure

[29]Indianapolis *Journal* and *Sentinel*, January 1-April 18, 1864, *passim*.
[30]*Official Records*, 2 series, VI, 878-80.

Sturgis, *Prisoners of War, 1861-65* (G. P. Putnam's Sons, 1912)

Camp Morton, 1864

for these cases, a proposal which was carried out and which apparently prevented any spread of the disease.[31]

A military prison was constructed about this time. It was a stout affair with walls, floors, ceiling, and doors of two thicknesses of two-inch planking, laid transversely to each other. It had four cells 15 feet square, ventilated by overhead gratings, a main prison room 24 by 30 feet, a dungeon 16 feet square, and an office and guardroom 12 by 24 feet. Sixty prisoners could be lodged there; there were thirty inmates in January, 1864, some of them Union bounty-jumpers awaiting court-martial. Three of these men, found guilty of repeated desertions, were executed on the parade ground near Camp Morton.[32]

Prisoners in the general barracks were still wretchedly clothed and quartered. Those who had no change of clothing could scarcely be expected to wash their only garments or bathe often in near-zero temperature, and vermin flourished among them. The plague drove some of the more fastidious prisoners to band together for the purchase of top bunks where the little beasts swarmed less profusely; occasionally, for the common good, a prisoner was forcibly bathed and shaved by his associates.[33]

Strict policing would have helped to keep the barracks free of other nuisances, and the prisoners would have been better off for some regular occupation, but Stevens had not roused their co-operative spirit. "Colonel Stevens is intelligent, of good habits, and competent to fill the position he occupies," said one inspector, "but does not fully understand the proper management of the prisoners."[34]

Lacking any camp duties, prisoners devoted themselves to plans for escape. They tried everything, singly and in groups, but Stevens' Veteran Reserves kept a strict watch. Two men

[31]*Official Records*, 2 series, VI, 992; Indianapolis *Sentinel*, February 15, 1864, p. 3, c. 1.

[32]Indianapolis *Journal*, January 28, 1864, p. 3, c. 1; Indianapolis *Sentinel*, January 29, 1864, p. 3, c. 1; Terrell, *Report*, I, Appendix, p. 287.

[33]*Official Records*, 2 series, VII, 71, 95-96; Wyeth, "Cold Cheer at Camp Morton," in *Century Magazine*, XLI, 852.

[34]*Official Records*, 2 series, VII, 71.

managed to evade the guard in November, and a member of the Twenty-seventh Louisiana died trying. In December, the intense cold helped to keep the record clear of escapes; in January three men were lucky enough to get away, and another man was shot in the attempt.[35]

Hoffman suggested to Stevens the advisability of employing detectives to ferret out plans for escape and to uncover communications between the prisoners and "ill-disposed persons outside."[36] This was doubtless a reference to the Sons of Liberty, once again active in Indiana, Illinois, and Ohio. Stevens already had some informants in the camp, but they were not omniscient, and the prisoners were resourceful.

One of the lucky ones was a young Texan about twenty years old who had been at Camp Morton since October, and had had his fill of northern winter. The slow tunneling process did not appeal to his temperament. He made a ladder of sorts from bits of wood and odds and ends of cloth, and concealed it in his bunk until one night when falling snow kept the sentinels blinking and blurred the sharp lights above the enclosure. At a moment when two sentries were farthest from each other on their beat, the ladder was flung across the top of the smooth high wall. A scramble, and the young Texan was over. The ladder slid back, and under a quick drift of snow remained undiscovered until the young man was safely on his way to Kentucky.[37]

Goacin Arcemont was unlucky. He came from Louisiana, and like the Texan, he hated the stinging northern winter. At one thirty in the morning of January 16 he slipped out of his barracks by a door that was not supposed to be used, and headed for an angle of the enclosure where prisoners had got safely away before. Challenged by the guard and ordered back to quarters, he stopped, but he did not turn back. He knew well enough what would follow a refusal to obey the second challenge, but perhaps he did not care very much. The guard repeated his order. Despairing or stubborn, Arcemont

[35]*Post*, p. 379; Indianapolis *Sentinel*, November 2, 1863, p. 3, c. 1; Indianapolis *Journal*, November 16, 1863, p. 3, c. 1, 2; November 19, p. 3, c. 3.

[36]*Official Records*, 2 series, VI, 893.

[37]Wyeth, "Cold Cheer at Camp Morton," in *Century Magazine*, XLI, 849.

stayed where he was, and after a little pause the guard fired, inflicting a wound of which the prisoner died.[38]

This occurrence brought from Hoffman a demand for a detailed account of the affair, based on an investigation made by Stevens himself. Were the prisoners fully apprised of the rules? What was the interval between the guard's second order and the shot? Who, beside the guard, gave evidence about the case? There must be no room for charges by the Confederacy that prisoners were shot down on trifling pretexts. Although Stevens was able to assure him that the guard had observed every requirement in this particular case, Hoffman sent an order to all camp commanders on March 17, 1864, requiring that a board of officers be summoned to investigate every case involving the shooting of a prisoner by a sentinel, and reiterating his warning against any excesses or cruelties.[39]

The prisoners meanwhile shut their eyes to the odds against successful escape and continued to plot. Two scaled the wall early in February. A few days later, ten men in Barracks G, near the fence, decided to tunnel out. They boarded up the side of a bunk, explaining to the guard that the muddy feet of men climbing to the bunks above dirtied their blankets. Behind this shield went the dirt dug on the first night. Next night, the refuse from the tunnel was lodged in the topmost bunk across the aisle. On the third night they devoted all their time to digging and none to concealment. Between three and four o'clock in the morning of February 11, they opened the tunnel outside the enclosure, beneath, and concealed by, the guards' walk. Due to this fortuitous point of exit, all of the original plotters except one who lost heart at the last minute emerged safely, taking with them two prisoners from other quarters.[40]

[38]Indianapolis *Sentinel*, January 19, 1864, p. 3, c. 1; *Official Records, 2 series*, VI, 884-85, 911-12, 941-42.

[39]*Ibid.*, VI, 911-12, 1073.

[40]Colonel Stevens and two of the prisoners involved, have left accounts of this escape. The story told by J. T. Branch in the *Confederate Veteran*, VIII, 71-72 (February, 1900) is the most circumstantial. See also article by J. J. Montgomery, in *ibid.*, VII, 10-12 (January, 1899), and Stevens' report, *Official Records, 2 series*, VI, 1043-44.

Word of the escape was whispered about the camp all day. So far as the prisoners knew, the tunnel had not been discovered, and there was a chance that it could be used again from Barracks G. In other parts of the camp excited prisoners laid plans to rush the wall. That night the two groups made a concerted try for freedom, but Stevens had been warned that a break was likely, and extra guards were stationed at vulnerable sections of the enclosure. One man was shot as he emerged from the tunnel, cutting off that route of escape, and musket fire thwarted the stampede against the wall. A few prisoners managed to get over the fence in the uproar, but some of them were recaptured; as a general uprising, the venture failed dismally.[41]

During the rigid inspection of the barracks that followed, another tunnel was found opening from Barracks A, and within a month four tunnels were discovered elsewhere in the camp.[42] Guards were put under the strictest orders to prevent further escapes—a hard assignment. All the prisoners were restless and defiant, although the more intelligent continued to shield their plans behind a front of good behavior. The stupid and vicious showed less foresight, making trouble among their comrades and insulting guards and officials openly. To send a stone cracking against a sentinel's cartridge box and spin him into an awkward about-face yielded a malicious joy that these men would not forego even to help their chances of escape. Stevens considered some of them "as tough and depraved characters" as he had ever seen, nevertheless, guards were commanded never to answer an insult and never to use force unless violence threatened.[43] Most of the Reserves had enough self-control to comply with the order, but a few were irritated into acts of brutality that no amount of provocation could justify.

Several prisoners were punished for attempted escape by

[41]*Official Records,* 2 series, VI, 946-47; Indianapolis *Journal,* February 15, 1864, p. 3, c. 1; February 19, p. 3, c. 2; Indianapolis *Sentinel,* February 15, 1864, p. 3, c. 2; February 20, p. 3, c. 1.

[42]*Official Records,* 2 series, VI, 946-47, 1044.

[43]"Treatment of Prisoners at Camp Morton," in *Century Magazine,* XLII, 768, 769.

having their arms fastened behind a tree while they marked time hour after hour; at least once, a culprit was tied up by the thumbs until he fainted from exhaustion. Other cruelties are said to have taken place with even less excuse: men were held unnecessarily long at roll call in freezing weather; a youngster was kicked and beaten for trying to secure an extra jacket when clothing was being issued; there were unauthorized shootings into the barracks—one prisoner who made a light after taps in order to help a sick comrade was shot, had to have his arm amputated, and died as a result. When these charges came into controversy, their truth was testified to by numbers of prisoners and in some cases by camp officials. Apparently most of the blame was attributable to one or two bullies among the noncommissioned officers; other guards and officials were absolved of responsibility even by the prisoners.[44]

[44]The Indianapolis newspapers contain very little information about what was going on at Camp Morton at this time, aside from one or two articles about the abnormally cold weather and mentions of the arrival and departure of prisoners. Outsiders were rigidly excluded from the camp. The reports of harsh treatment were first publicized in April, 1891, when John A. Wyeth, prisoner at Camp Morton from October, 1863 to February, 1865, and later a physician of repute and president of the American Medical Association, wrote an article for *Century Magazine* (XLI, 844-52) called "Cold Cheer at Camp Morton." It painted a dark picture, and was received with great indignation in Indiana. In November, 1891, it was answered by W. W. Holloway, Governor Morton's secretary during the war, in a statement which *Century* printed (XLII, 757-70) together with a rejoinder by Wyeth (*ibid.*, 771-75). Each side offered much supporting testimony, Holloway to the effect that the charges were indefensible and malicious, and Wyeth to show that he had exaggerated nothing. Much of the material in these articles was reviewed by James R. Carnahan, of the Indianapolis Commandery, Loyal Legion, in a defense of Camp Morton, printed in 1892, while numerous articles upholding Wyeth's assertions appeared in the *Confederate Veteran*. In 1914 Dr. Wyeth retold his story as a chapter in a volume called *With Sabre and Scalpel*. A comparison of this chapter with his first article shows some modifications, based on the replies of Holloway and Carnahan, and on the eight volumes of *Official Records* dealing with prisoners of war (these volumes began to appear in 1894) but in the essentials he sticks to his original story. At those points where the *Official Records* cover the matters of which he speaks—for example, the condition of barracks, hospitals, and clothing issues—they tend to substantiate his statements. For material on the charges cited in the text, see Wyeth, "Cold Cheer at Camp Morton," in *Century Magazine*, XLI, 849, 850-51; "Treatment of Prisoners at Camp Morton," in *Century Magazine*, XLII, 768, 772-74.

Harsh treatment may have cowed some of the weaker spirits, but it was not, generally, effective in preventing escapes. Other measures worked far better. Stevens ordered twenty feet taken off the end of the barracks nearest the fence, and started the prisoners digging a trench within the walls so wide and deep that tunneling below it would be practically impossible. The Confederates regarded this occupation with extreme disfavor, as might be expected, but the work went on, and when the job was finished, a stout board enclosure was erected inside the old wall as a further barrier against unauthorized departures.[45]

In late February, 1864, a squabble between Hoffman and Major General Benjamin F. Butler, who had been made a special agent of exchange, did the prisoners a good turn. Butler found his attempts to supply comforts to Union prisoners coldly received by the Confederates because Hoffman was refusing to allow the delivery of boxes of provisions to southern prisoners. Exasperated by this inept management, Butler wrote to Colonel Hoffman in the tone of a sarcastic headmaster addressing a clumsy schoolboy. Hoffman's comment that the delivery of packages caused a great deal of trouble to the prison commandants especially provoked him, since it was obvious that a little more effort on the part of these gentlemen would work as much to the advantage of Union as of Confederate prisoners.[46]

"I desire to have and shall have the delivery of packages made in accordance with the views herein contained," announced Butler, "unless specifically directed to the contrary by the Secretary of War." Hoffman forwarded the letter to Stanton, and with it requests from the commandant at Camp Chase for permission to extend the list of articles which might be sold to prisoners of war. It was decided that the exchange of provisions be allowed on a reciprocity basis, and that a sutler be appointed in each camp.[47]

[45]*Official Records,* 2 series, VI, 946-47, 1044; VII, 95; Indianapolis *Journal,* March 21, 1864, p. 3, c. 1; March 28, p. 3, c. 2; Indianapolis *Sentinel,* June 22, 1864, p. 3, c. 1.
[46]*Official Records,* 2 series, VI, 954-55, 973-75; VIII, 343.
[47]*Ibid.,* VI, 983-85.

Boxes "containing nothing hurtful or contraband" were thereafter delivered at the camps. Military equipment and intoxicating liquors were among the contraband articles, and clothing was not allowed in excess of "immediate" requirements. This last stricture was narrowly construed. For instance, one destitute prisoner who appealed to his family for a new outfit got only a shirt and pantaloons, a pair of socks, and a pair of shoes out of a package which contained a coat, hat, another shirt, and extra socks in addition.[48]

Prisoners did their best to get around the antiliquor rule. Wines and whiskies kept in the hospital storeroom had an irresistible attraction for an orderly named Whitehead. He discovered in the storeroom ceiling a hole intended to accommodate a stovepipe, and by means of a lasso was able to fish out a bottle of liquor every now and then. For a while occasional breakages in the locked room were attributed to mice and rats, as he had hoped, but a suspicious surgeon eventually set a watch on the place, and Whitehead found himself repining the loss of his "bitters" in the guardhouse.[49]

The new regulations for sutlers, issued on March 3, were sensible and generous. No sales were to be made before eight o'clock or after half an hour before sundown, when they would obviously interfere with camp routine. The stock was to be restricted to certain articles—a fairly comprehensive list which would have allowed the prisoner (always providing that he had funds) to enlarge his supply of shoes, socks, and underclothes, and supplement his rations with fruit, vegetables, and other nourishing foods.[50]

It does not appear that Stevens applied the rules strictly. The first report mentioning the sutler at Camp Morton states that he was selling pies, cakes, soda water, and candies, but whether these articles were in addition to those on Hoffman's list or a poor substitute for them, is not clear. A new circular covering the treatment of prisoners of war, issued on April

[48]*Ibid.*, VI, 1036; VII, 75; "Treatment of Prisoners at Camp Morton," in *Century Magazine*, XLII, 774.
[49]Indianapolis *Sentinel,* November 2, 1863, p. 3, c. 2.
[50]*Official Records,* 2 series, VI, 1014, 1036.

20, 1864, required that sutlers be obliged to furnish the prescribed articles at reasonable prices. The sutler was to pay a small tax, which was to become a part of the prisoners' fund.[51]

The circular of April 20 also carried a new ruling about rations. Whereas until this time the amount of the regular army rations that might be withheld from the prisoners and commuted into a prisoners' fund had been left to the judgment of the camp commandants, this order made a flat schedule for all prison depots.[52] Whether the new allowance was more or less than the issue then in effect at Camp Morton does not appear; it is probable that it was less, for inspectors had never criticised the quantity of food furnished there, although they had found plenty of fault with the shortage of vegetables and the poor cooking arrangements.

At least one camp commander considered the new ration too small, but the commander of big Camp Douglas wrote to Hoffman that he thought it could be reduced still further. He recommended doing away with hominy, tea, and candles, on the grounds that the hominy was almost entirely wasted, tea was unnecessary, and the candles had been used chiefly "in tunneling or in studying up some other means of escape."[53]

Hoffman welcomed the suggestion. Since dispatching the circular of April 20, he had made a visit to Annapolis to oversee the reception of some paroled Union soldiers brought North by truce boat. He found most of the officers in good health and happy, but the condition of the enlisted men returning from Belle Isle Prison horrified him, and caused him to discredit the Confederate claim that prisoners were receiving army rations. Reports from Andersonville, established in December, 1863, were also distilling bitterness. On May 3, 1864, Hoffman wrote to Stanton advocating retaliation on the officers in northern prisons, and on the nineteenth he wrote again, proposing a general reduction in prison rations. His proposal was approved by Stanton, Halleck, the Acting Surgeon General, and the Commissary General of Subsistence, and on

[51]*Official Records*, 2 series, VII, 71, 74.
[52]*Ibid.*, VI, 1081; *post*, p. 381.
[53]*Official Records*, 2 series, VII, 134, 142-43.

June 1 was incorporated in a circular and transmitted to prison commanders.[54]

Candles and molasses had disappeared from the allowance completely; bread was reduced from 18 to 16 ounces per day, potatoes from 30 pounds to 15 pounds per hundred men, and the salt portion was lessened. Sugar and coffee or tea were removed from the ration of all but the sick and wounded; the latter were allowed small amounts every other day.[55] From the dietary angle, the worst feature of the measure was the reduction of potatoes and salt; from the prisoners' point of view, the regulation best exemplifying Yankee hatefulness was the withdrawal of the daily cup of coffee.

Stevens received the order with misgivings. For one thing, the temper of the camp had been increasingly inflamed ever since the shooting of two prisoners a few weeks before. Several prisoners had been detailed to help with the disposal of garbage. While they were marching along behind the wagon, followed by an excitable and inexperienced guard, two of them stepped out of line and ran up beside the wagon. According to the guard's story, he ordered them to fall back, and at the same time brought his musket to "Charge bayonets," cocking it with his thumb as he brought it down. In his excitement the musket was discharged, and the two men in the path of the bullet were fatally wounded. The guard was arrested, tried for murder, and acquitted, but many of the prisoners were convinced that the shooting had been intentional, and continued to look upon the guard as nothing better than an assassin.[56]

Investigations made by General Carrington were also disturbing. Stevens was convinced that the Sons of Liberty now had contacts within the camp, and that designs were being laid to promote an uprising. To add to his uneasiness, the

[54]*Official Records,* 2 series, VII, 110-11, 150-51, 183-84. A somewhat larger ration was established on June 13 for prisoners employed on public works. *Ibid.,* VII, 366-67.

[55]*Post,* p. 381.

[56]Wyeth, "Cold Cheer at Camp Morton," in *Century Magazine,* XLI, 849-50; Carnahan, *Camp Morton,* 40-41; "Treatment of Prisoners at Camp Morton," in *Century Magazine,* XLII, 773, 774.

prisoners' strength had been increased by six hundred men sent North in May; more were expected.[57] To reduce rations was to invite an explosion. Additional safeguards were demanded, and General Carrington procured a howitzer battery from St. Louis, which was placed to protect the angles of the fence.[58]

Introduction of the short ration met the belligerent reception that Stevens expected. "I have just returned from Camp Morton, where there are indications of attempted revolt of the prisoners," wrote Carrington on June 4.[59] "Last night stones had been collected in large numbers and tunnels had been pushed forward to considerable progress. They have destroyed some of their utensils and talk defiantly. A portion of the excitement grew out of reduction of rations. To-day the issue of coffee ceases.

"The officers and guard are on the alert and will be doubled to-night. The force is inadequate for the duty devolved upon them, and lumber is greatly needed for necessary repairs. I have ordered an inspection of the prison."

The threatening muzzles of the howitzer battery and the doubled guard held the prisoners in check temporarily, and Stevens turned his attention to providing accommodations for extra prisoners.

[57]Indianapolis *Sentinel,* May 23, 1864, p. 3, c. 1 ; May 27, p. 3, c. 1 ; Indianapolis *Journal,* May 25, 1864, p. 3, c. 1.

[58]Terrell, *Report,* I, Appendix, 273 ; *Official Records,* 2 series, VII, 193.

[59]*Ibid.*

VII. THE LAST YEAR, 1864-65

CAMP MORTON housed 4,999 prisoners in July, 1864, a fifty per cent increase since the first of May: 609 had arrived late in that month, 1,350 in June, and 568 in July.[1] Renovations and improvements at the camp had not been made on a scale to accommodate half the newcomers. By the end of July the seven barracks housed from 436 to 484 inmates each, 554 men occupied the old cattle shed, and a fourth of the men were still sweltering in tents set in cramped rows between the buildings. Fortunately kitchens had at last been erected, in each of which cooking was done for from three to four hundred prisoners; this was a great reform, but its good effects were reduced by the omission of succulent vegetables from the diet. Beef cooked in quantity might taste better and go further, but it did not prevent scurvy.[2]

The advent of July was dreaded by the camp physicians. The hot days brought deadly exhalations from the earth, trampled by thousands of men and impregnated with filth, while the sink, situated near the center of the camp, spread its noxious gases broadcast. July was the month too when malaria began to seize its victims. Even in 1863, when the number of prisoners was below a thousand, the death rate during that month had been high. In 1864, the camp was swarming, and matters were made still worse by heat as blistering as the winter cold had been severe. Three cases of sunstroke in downtown Indianapolis were reported by the *Sentinel* of June 21. Later issues commented in a depressed fashion on the succession of burning days, and by July 23 wells and cisterns had begun to go dry.[3]

The hospitals were soon full. One building had been remodeled to contain the office and dispensary, storerooms, and a kitchen and messroom, while the wards had become such

[1] *Post,* p. 379.
[2] *Official Records,* 2 series, VII, 512-13, 554.
[3] *Ibid.*

"models of neatness" that a sojourn there was regarded as the best thing the camp had to offer.[4] The patients were better clothed and better fed than the men outside, and behind Surgeon Kipp's professional ability they perceived a heart-warming personal interest. Kipp had efficient assistants, too.[5] His worst foes were the intolerably crowded quarters and a general debility which complicated every case of illness. Following a week when twenty-four of his patients died, he was requested to make a statement of the causes to Surgeon Charles J. Tripler, Medical Director of the Northern Department. His reply showed plainly that no improvement could be expected as long as the prisoners remained in cramped quarters and were denied antiscorbutics.[6]

With Tripler's strong endorsement, the statement eventually reached Hoffman's hands. It was reinforced almost immediately by a report from Medical Inspector Alexander, who visited Camp Morton on August 5 and 6.[7] He said bluntly that the number of sick—327 in hospital and 256 in barracks—was out of proportion to the number of prisoners, and recommended (1) enlargement of the camp; (2) building of eight hospital wards in the added area; (3) conversion of existing hospital wards into quarters; (4) reconstruction of the cattle shed into a barracks by the addition of another half; (5) a free supply of vegetables for the next two months; (6) improved police.

All this he thought could be done at less than the cost of replacing 198 worn-out tents still in use but unfit for winter occupancy. He himself had instituted measures to improve the sinks, and had ordered onions supplied from the prison fund, which amounted to $36,215.52 at the end of July.

Hoffman was impressed into instituting the reforms that could be handled without much expense. Antiscorbutics were issued regularly thereafter—half a pound of potatoes or six

[4]*Official Records,* 2 series, VII, 94.

[5]*Ibid.,* VII, 556. Five acting assistant surgeons of the U. S. Army were now on duty at Camp Morton. They were R. N. Todd, W. P. Parr, I. N. Craig, W. S. Thompson, and S. C. Dove.

[6]*Ibid.,* VII, 512-13, 554-56.

[7]*Ibid.,* VII, 554-56.

ounces of onions per man. Stevens was ordered to take into the enclosure about ten acres at the northeast corner, and to report weekly on the condition of the camp.[8] He appointed Lieutenant J. W. Davidson, of the Veteran Reserve Corps, to act as camp inspector and see that policing was regular and thorough.

After examining the noisome barracks, Davidson characterized the prisoners as "the filthiest set of men in the world." They obstructed his every move, but they could not balk this stubborn officer. As soon as the barracks were empty in the morning, a detail of prisoners was assigned to give them a sweeping. Bedding was then aired and rolled neatly at the head of each bunk, in regular army camp fashion. The men were inspected, too, and anyone who came dirty to the morning line-up was taken from the ranks and washed.[9]

Davidson had scarcely had time to admire the results when Hoffman, in a fit of economy, threatened to reduce the soap ration. Davidson saw his charges slipping back into their former grimy state, and protested with an earnestness that gave no thought to the niceties of grammar: "The rations of soap, I have found, is not more than is required, owing to the water that has to be used for washing being of such a nature as to require a large quantity to enable them to keep themselves and their clothing clean."[10]

Other reforms recommended by Inspector Alexander bogged down because Hoffman and Stevens got at cross purposes over requisitions and authorizations. As an illustration of the disastrous results produced in the prison camps by false economy and red tape, the struggle to improve accommodations for the winter of 1864-65 will be followed in some detail.

The whole plan to provide barrack room for the men in

[8]*Official Records, 2* series, VII, 585, 599.

[9]*Ibid.,* VII, 693, 771, 843; Indianapolis *Journal,* October 25, 1864, p. 1, c. 4-5. Davidson has been accused of tyrannical and cruel behavior toward the prisoners (*Confederate Veteran,* XV, 223-26. May, 1907), and his reports sometimes betray extreme exasperation at their unhelpfulness. On the other hand, his efforts to secure better quarters for them were unremitting.

[10]*Official Records, 2* series, VII, 599, 694. Stevens reported that 5,495½ pounds of soap, and 1,030½ gallons of vinegar were required in August. *Ibid.,* VII, 824.

tents and reduce the crowding in the regular quarters hinged on the building of enough new hospital wards to accommodate all the sick, and release the old wards for conversion into barracks. Perhaps Stevens did not emphasize this point sufficiently when he forwarded the recommendations of his subordinates. Kipp had added several details to the suggestions already made. He wanted windows in the barracks, bunks limited to two tiers instead of three, an "ablution room" attached to each building, and a messroom to each kitchen.[11] It was impossible to keep the barracks clean in winter when the men had to eat indoors. Davidson begged for the construction of floors in the barracks, partly as a sanitary measure, and partly to make tunneling more difficult. He was distressed about the men in leaky tents, and harped on the necessity of providing better quarters for them before cold weather.[12] Stevens unfortunately neglected to provide estimates of costs, a fatal omission in dealing with Hoffman.

As the days went by without word from Washington, Stevens revised his plans and began makeshift repairs with materials on hand. By remodeling an extension of the cattle shed along the north wall, brought inside the enclosure by the enlargement of the grounds, it was possible to take 585 men out of tents. The most dilapidated tents were then discarded and the rest moved to fresh ground.[13] Beyond improvements of this sort Stevens was unwilling to go without authorization from Washington.

When Hoffman finally wrote to Stevens on September 14, he did not mention the barracks at all, and he criticized the proposals for the hospital as too elaborate. Instead of authorizing the construction of the six or eight wards needed, he ordered the building of two. Specifications were to be as follows:[14]

Dimensions, 25 feet by 110, with 9 1/2 feet elevation from the floor; clothes room, bathing room, and closet in each ward; eight windows in a side at intervals of 11 feet, allowing three beds between; one row of beds to run lengthwise, providing

[11]*Official Records*, 2 series, VII, 663-64.
[12]*Ibid.*, VII, 693-94, 771, 812, 843, 918.
[13]*Ibid.*
[14]*Ibid.*, VII, 823.

accommodations for fifty men to a ward. A building 20 by 60 feet was authorized for the kitchen and messroom, and another, 24 by 75 feet, to contain a room for the surgeon, an office, dispensary, storeroom, and a room for attendants. The buildings were to be put up without framing, the posts set in the ground and the joists spiked to them. Felt roofing was recommended as warmer than shingles, and floors were to be elevated one foot above the ground. Stevens was asked to report on the costs as soon as the wards were completed.

Materials had to be assembled before work could begin, and construction was further delayed by heavy rains. Hoffman, waiting to hear how the hospital wards were progressing, got nothing but Davidson's weekly pleas for better barracks. Irritated and impatient, he wrote to Stevens on October 3 scoring these "vague suggestions" and "recommendations without details."[15]

Stevens replied patiently with a statement of what he had done and what he hoped to do. By October 20 the hospital wards were finished, and reporting this fact, Stevens brought up once again the need for at least four more.[16] Expense was not prohibitive, for the first two cost but $915.46, and the prison fund was climbing steadily.[17] Hoffman received the suggestion as though it were brand new. "If the tents now in use can possibly be made to serve . . . this winter, no further buildings will be erected; but if the tents are wholly unfit for further use, you are authorized to erect additional hospital wards and convert the present hospital into barracks, as you recommend. Report what you think proper to do in this matter."[18] If Stevens read this communication with anger and frustration, who can blame him? For weeks he had been reporting the measures that he considered necessary, and his reports had been backed up by recommendations of the camp inspector, the camp surgeon, and the district medical inspector.

[15]*Ibid.*, VII, 919.

[16]*Ibid.*, VII, 927-28, 1034.

[17]*Ibid.*, VII, 1166. In December, 1864, the prison fund amounted to about $75,000. Alvin P. Hovey to The Adjutant General, December 2, 1864. Photostat, Indiana Division, Indiana State Library.

[18]*Official Records*, 2 series, VII, 1069-70.

Shortly after this, on November 11, Hoffman was made Commissary General of Prisoners West of the Mississippi, a position which he held until February 1, 1865. For that period he was replaced at Washington by Brigadier General Henry W. Wessells. Immediately, Stevens' communications began to receive consideration, but so much time had been wasted already in fruitless correspondence that the camp was doomed to face another winter ill prepared.

Construction of additional hospital wards, approved by Wessells' office on November 21, was retarded by snow and ice; before they were completed it was plain that they would not suffice (on December 29, Surgeon Kipp had room for 240 patients and a daily sick report of 400, many of the patients coming from the group of prisoners who were still living in tents). Kipp begged for three more wards and toward the end of January, 1865, received permission to build them with prison labor.[19]

What the months of haggling over hospitals and winter quarters cost is told by the prisoners' death rolls: September, 1864, 33; October, 21; November, 18; December, 53; January, 1865, 117; February, 133.[20]

Life at Camp Morton from the summer of 1864 to the spring of 1865 followed the pattern of the preceding year in other aspects. On August 10, 1864, Hoffman once more prohibited sutlers from selling food to prisoners of war, and so restricted the delivery of boxes from their families as virtually to cut off that source of supplies. Sutlers still furnished tobacco, stamps, and odds and ends of toilet and sewing articles, and some of them did a little smuggling on the side. The Camp Morton sutler, Dwight Roberts, was charged with selling small gingerbread cakes worth about two cents each to agents among the prisoners at the rate of eleven cakes for a dollar; the agents then tacked on a big profit for themselves, and the hungry consumer had to pay fifteen or twenty-five cents for his illicit bite of gingerbread. Another sharp practice was to force the prisoners to buy at least thirty

[19]*Official Records*, 2 series, VII, 1102-3, 1117, 1128, 1154-55, 1166, 1202, 1211, 1242, 1294; VIII, 134, 144.
[20]*Post*, p. 379.

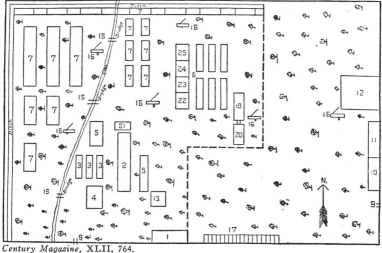

CAMP MORTON, 1865 (Compiled from sketches by several persons who were on duty in the camp). 1. Headquarters. 2. Old hospital. 3. Hospital tents. 4. Sutler. 5. Hospitals—built in 1863. 6. New hospitals—built in 1864. 7. Barracks. 9. Gates. 10. Quartermaster. 11. Commissary. 12. Bakery. 13. Baseball grounds. 15. Bridges. 16. Pumps. 17. Sheds, officers' horses. 19. Dining room. 20. Kitchen. 21. Dining room. 22. Consulting room. 23. Reception room. 24. Engineer. 25. Prescription, supplies. - - - Guard line.

cents worth of provisions at a time or forfeit the change due from a sutler's check worth a dollar.[21] As will appear later, the prisoners found a way of avenging themselves.

Food gradually became the center of men's thoughts, the subject of most of their conversations, and the basis of a strange camp commerce. Chief commodities in camp trading operations were bread ("duffers"), crackers ("hardtack"), beef bones, and bone butter, and the unit of currency was a "chaw" of tobacco, cut to a standard size of an inch square and a quarter inch thick. Bone butter rated as the top luxury on the prison bill of fare. If a man drew a beef joint on his

[21]*Official Records*, 2 series, VII, 573-74; letter of James A. Edwards to "the Proper Officer," Washington, D. C., February 27, 1865, photostat, Archives Division, Indiana State Library, from War Department, Letters Received, Secretary of War.

ration he had the makings of this delicacy and was happy. The meat was scraped off and cooked. The bone was then split into very small pieces and boiled until all the fat was extracted and the water evaporated. After the residue had been filtered through a cloth and allowed to harden, the bone butter was ready—and worth a big price in camp currency.

In fair weather the dealers had a regular market place; on rainy days they made their rounds through the barracks. Almost everybody joined in the daily bargaining. It was an occupation that relieved the terrible ennui of the long days and provided a momentary defense against nostalgia.[22]

Some men found their entertainment in gambling. Since rations were the usual stake the game was exciting, but the losers had to choose between starving like gentlemen or obtaining food by irregular means. Rat eating was not uncommon during the period of short rations: there was no stigma attached to the practice. When the sutler's dog went the way of the rats, however, some of the prisoners invited to the vengeful feast could not bring themselves to share it. A few men were driven to the extremity of filching scraps from the hospital garbage, but their comrades soon formed a committee to prevent this degrading practice. They also held court on the rascals who stole from their comrades.[23]

Early in August, 1864, the prisoners' clothing was described as bad and deficient. There were some reserves in the quartermaster's department, but not enough to last through the winter. Late in the month, Lieutenant Davidson asked for 530 woolen blankets, 825 pairs of trousers, 1,250 pairs of shoes, 850 shirts, and 350 coats, and took the trouble to point out that most of the 4,800 prisoners at Camp Morton were too poor to secure outfits from home. The supplies arrived slowly—there was still a shortage of shoes on October 18— and later more shirts and blankets had to be requisitioned. In December, Davidson

[22]Wyeth, "Cold Cheer at Camp Morton," in *Century Magazine,* XLI, 851-52.

[23]*Ibid.,* 848, 851; "Plain Living at Johnson's Island," in *Century Magazine,* XLI, 715; "Treatment of Prisoners at Camp Morton," in *Century Magazine,* XLII, 765, 774, 775; *Official Records,* 2 series, VIII, 347, 348.

asked that straw be furnished for bedding as the prisoners did not have enough blankets.[24]

In the meantime a plan was being worked out under which the Federal Government was to furnish Union men in southern prisons with food, clothing and blankets, shelter and fuel, and hospital stores, while the Confederacy supplied its men in the North. To secure funds, the South was allowed to ship cotton for sale in New York.[25] Brigadier General William N. R. Beall, a prisoner at Fort Warren, was paroled on December 6 to take charge of the sale, make the necessary purchases, and manage the distribution. The cotton came late (January 24, 1865) and in such bad condition that it had to be rebaled. It was sold on February 8, and by the tenth Beall had made his purchases. To the dismay of General Halleck, not a cent was spent for provisions: every penny went for tobacco and for shoes, gray blankets, and clothing that was "in every respect the Confederate uniform (save the buttons)." Since exchanges were once more under way, this looked like an attempt to outfit the men for the field, and the North refused to extend its agreement to cover further sales of cotton.[26]

General Beall's purchases were distributed in February. Prisoners at Camp Morton received as their share 12 packages of tobacco, 1,500 blankets, 1,580 coats and jackets, 1,585 pairs of trousers, 1,730 shirts, 1,600 drawers, 1,800 pairs of socks, and 800 pairs of shoes.[27] This was an impressive issue in comparison with the quantities asked for by Lieutenant Davidson, and leaves the unhappy conviction that coats and blankets at the camp were far too few from November to February.

During the summer and autumn of 1864 liberation of prisoners again became an important objective of forlorn-hope Confederates and hotheaded leaders of the Sons of Liberty in the North. Their extravagant scheme contemplated the over-

[24]*Official Records,* 2 series, VII, 694, 785, 843, 927, 966, 1007-8, 1147, 1166, 1211.

[25]*Ibid.,* VII, 1070-73, 1107-8. It was part of the agreement that no article furnished by either Government should be "upon any pretense or for any cause whatever, diverted from the use" for which it was dedicated.

[26]*Ibid.,* VII, 1117-18, 1131, 1148-49, 1199-1200; VIII, 124, 227, 241-42.
[27]*Ibid.,* VIII, 318, 750.

throw of the state governments of Missouri, Illinois, Indiana, and Ohio, and the occupation of Kentucky. Governor Morton was to be assassinated. The arsenals were to be seized and the prisoners freed and armed to join Confederate forces moving in from Missouri and Kentucky.

"Visionary and desperate as this scheme may appear," said one of Morgan's ablest officers later, "it was in reality very nearly the last hope the South had of prolonging the war. She had exhausted every other means of recruiting her fearfully depleted armies. Much of her territory had been overrun and no longer furnished either men or supplies to the Confederate cause. Enlistment in the territory still under Confederate control had almost ceased; indeed, the material for it had scarcely any longer existence. The conscription, no matter how rigorously enforced, brought no acquisition to the ranks, simply because it could not find men capable of serving. Nowhere, except among the great army of her veterans cooped up in Northern prisons, could the South find the men who, with their remaining comrades yet in the field and standing desperately at bay, might still fight her battles and prolong the struggle."[28]

So much for the position of the South. But the plan went far beyond anything dreamed of by most northern members of the order. Shocked and alienated by its treasonable aspects, many withdrew in Indiana. Others succeeded in postponing action in the state, and the plan for a rising in August collapsed with the seizure of a shipment of arms—labeled Sunday school books—at the office of H. H. Dodd, Grand Commander for Indiana, and his subsequent arrest.[29] Some of his agents were sent to the military prison at Camp Morton.

General Carrington reported that papers found in Dodd's office included a list of four hundred prisoners of war who were members of the Sons of Liberty, and that he had learned from some of the prisoners that two thousand of their number

[28]General Basil W. Duke, in Introduction to John B. Castleman's *Active Service* (Louisville, Kentucky, 1917).

[29]Terrell, *Report*, I, 299 ff.; Indianapolis *Journal*, August 22, 1864, p. 2, c. 1-5; August 23, p. 1, c. 5-8, p. 2, c. 1-2; *Official Records*, VII, 801-3, 930-53, 1089.

had organized battalions and chosen leaders in preparation for an outbreak. Dodd denied that any prisoners were members of the order, but he was quoted at his trial in September as having said that with 150 men he could seize the artillery at Camp Morton and overpower the guards, and there was ample evidence that he expected the prisoners to co-operate in the general uprising.[30]

Although these plans came to nothing, they kept the officials at Camp Morton uneasy and doubly watchful. Additional guards were brought in, the Sixtieth Massachusetts Volunteer Infantry, and the Thirty-seventh Iowa Volunteers both assisting the Fifth and Seventeenth Regiments of Veteran Reserves. The prisoners immediately recognized inexperienced guards and tried to make capital of the situation. On August 17 eight of them who had been sent outside the camp on fatigue duty overpowered their guard. Six escaped, one was recaptured, and one came back to camp of his own accord. A month later a prisoner tried to get away from a similar fatigue party and was killed.[31] Informants within the camp gave warning meanwhile that some of the prisoners were perfecting plans for an attack on the enclosure, and were determined to fight their way to the arsenals no matter what the cost of life.[32]

Dozens of tunnels were discovered; some progressed for weeks before betrayal or mischance called them to the guards' attention. One of these was begun two hundred feet from the prison wall. A ten-foot shaft was sunk, and two feet from the bottom of the shaft a cross trench was run parallel to the surface until it dipped underneath the ditch that Stevens had hoped would make tunneling impracticable.

[30]Carrington to Lieutenant Colonel S. H. Lathrop, August 24, 1864, photostat in Indiana Division, Indiana State Library, from War Department, Northern Department Letter Books, Vol. 69, pp. 88-89; Indianapolis *Sentinel,* September 5, 1864, p. 2, c. 4; September 28, p. 2, c. 4; October 26, p. 3, c. 2; *Official Records,* 2 series, VII, 947-48.

[31]Indianapolis *Sentinel,* August 11, 1864, p. 3, c. 1; August 18, p. 3, c. 1; August 19, p. 3, c. 1; August 24, p. 3, c. 1; September 19, p. 3, c. 1; Indianapolis *Journal,* August 19, 1864, p. 3, c. 1; *Official Records,* 2 series, VII, 911-12.

[32]Carrington to Lieutenant Colonel S. H. Lathrop, August 23, 1864, photostat in Indiana Division, Indiana State Library, from War Department, Northern Department, Letter Books, Vol. 69, p. 87.

Elaborate precautions were taken to keep the work secret. Some of the plotters were always at hand to blanket the shaft when a patrol appeared, and help disguise the opening by starting a card game on the covering. One man at a time worked inside the tunnel, digging with a case knife, and pushing the earth into a bag which was tied at the middle of a long cord and could be hauled back and forth in response to a signal from either end.

Before the prisoners went to their barracks at sundown the fresh earth was carefully disposed of. Each man tucked his trousers into his socks, filled them with "as much loose earth as he could waddle with," and made for the "Potomac." Reaching the middle of the plank bridge across the little stream, he gave his trousers a sudden pull, disengaging them from his stockings and allowing the dirt to slide into the stream, where the rapid current soon carried off all evidence of his burrowing.

On a September morning the plotters hugged the knowledge that the tunnel was ready to cut through; as the day wore on, fifteen of them realized with sick foreboding that the sixteenth man of the party had disappeared. A surreptitious search discovered their Judas—safe behind the guardlines at headquarters, where he remained until the end of the war.[33]

On the night of September 27 a more spectacular attempt at escape doubled the tension in the camp. Some time before, the fifteen or twenty prisoners involved had spliced together half a dozen ladders out of tent poles and the short ladders from their bunks; they had been waiting since for just such a night of rain and pitch darkness as closed over the camp on the twenty-seventh. It was in their favor, too, that part of the troops on guard that night were armed only with musket and bayonet, and could fire only once without reloading.

Letting fly a barrage of rocks and stones to draw the sentries' fire, the prisoners rushed the wall. "By God, I'm all right," shouted one as he reached the top, and was shot as he spoke. Another was fatally wounded. A few got over the fence and away; though little trails of blood indicated that

[33]Wyeth, "Cold Cheer at Camp Morton," in *Century Magazine*, XLI, 850.

some of them had suffered gunshot or bayonet wounds, none of them were recaptured, and it was supposed that they had found shelter with Confederate sympathizers.[34]

There were brought to Camp Morton on October 2 two of the young Confederate officers who had been trying to prod northern Sons of Liberty into aiding their plans. One was Lieutenant William E. Munford; the other was Captain John Breckenridge Castleman, of Louisville, Kentucky, who had been working with Captain Thomas H. Hines, already well known for his dashing foray into Indiana the preceding summer and his spectacular escape with General Morgan from the Ohio State Penitentiary at Columbus. Because they were traveling in civilian clothes and under assumed names when arrested, they were charged with spying, and were placed in close confinement in the Camp Morton prison.

Within a few days Castleman had induced a guard to bring him a saw, and had cut an opening in the floor of his cell large enough to allow him to slip out. A short inspection disclosed a close-set ring of sentinels around the prison and beyond them the high wall surrounding the enclosure. There was nothing to do but climb back into Cell 3 and replace the floorboards.

Castleman was treated with consideration. The officer in charge of the prison, Colonel A. J. Warner, of the Seventeenth Regiment Veteran Reserves, visited him frequently, and permitted him to have a private interview with his mother and to receive the Bible which she brought. The Bible had been supplied by Captain Hines and contained $3,000 in one side of the binding and a fine saw in the other, but Castleman was never able to engineer an escape. His Unionist brother-in-law, Judge Samuel Breckenridge, of St. Louis, saw President Lincoln secretly on his behalf in November, and received from him a note to be used only in case of emergency.

"Whenever John B. Castleman shall be tried, if convicted and sentenced, suspend execution until further order from me, and send me the record.

A. LINCOLN"

[34]*Official Records*, 2 series, VII, 915-16.

Castleman knew nothing of this, and during the next few months must have spent many hours contemplating the probable consequences if he were tried as a spy.[35]

Doubtless the Camp Morton grapevine carried through the enclosure the story of Castleman's errand in the North; the prisoners may have had secret knowledge, too, that Hines was still working to release the prisoners at Camp Douglas, knowledge that gave them courage for the last and most successful prison break of the season. On the night of November 14, just as the bugle was calling prisoners to their barracks, and before the night patrol had reached the prison yard, a mob of fifty or sixty men rushed toward the fence. Stones and bottles filled with water hurtled through the air at the guards, taking them so completely by surprise that only a few shots were fired. The prisoners bridged the ditch with an overturned shed and went over the fence like cats. Tumbling down the bank, they fled into the woods before reinforcements reached the disorganized guards. An all-night search party corralled a part of them, but thirty-one concealed themselves successfully and were seen no more at Camp Morton.[36]

There was wrath at the camp. Stevens and other officials had been asking for weeks for an efficient guard regiment to support the Fifth Veteran Reserves. The break justified their requests, but not in a manner pleasing to officialdom. It did result, however, in the replacement of the Sixtieth Massachusetts Volunteer Infantry by the Forty-third Indiana, and from that time on, but four men escaped from Camp Morton.[37]

One group of prisoners had been trying for many months to secure their release by amicable means. They were mostly Louisianans who had been captured in the Vicksburg campaign

---

[35]Castleman, *Active Service*, 147-48, 172-79; *Official Records*, 2 series, VIII, 704-5.

[36]Wyeth, "Cold Cheer at Camp Morton," in *Century Magazine*, XLI, 849; "Treatment of Prisoners at Camp Morton," in *Century Magazine*, XLII, 768; Alvin P. Hovey to Captain C. H. Potter, November 15, 1864, photostat, Indiana Division, Indiana State Library, from War Department, Northern Department Letter Books, Vol. 70, p. 100; *Official Records*, 2 series, VII, 1146.

[37]District Special Orders 175, November 16, 1864, Mereness Calendar, War Department, Northern Department Orders, Vol. 84, p. 39.

Sturgis, *Prisoners of War 1861-65* (G. P. Putnam's Sons, 1912)

Camp Morton, 1864

in July, 1863. Many of them had been conscripted into service and were not sorry to be taken prisoners. When offered parole on the field, they refused it, having got the impression from some source that they would be allowed to take the oath of allegiance to the Union and return home.

Instead of being sent to St. Louis or Memphis, given the oath and released, as they expected, they were sent to Camp Morton, and there they had remained. They kept themselves aloof from the other prisoners, and presently, under the leadership of Louis Lefebvre, began an agitation to secure their liberty. Stevens was impressed by their story and by their good behavior. He gave them what help he could, and allowed them to communicate with their New Orleans friends. In May, 1864, Governor Hahn of Louisiana petitioned for their discharge, and in July, Adjutant General Noble, of Indiana, wrote to Hoffman on their behalf. It was decided at Washington, however, that no exception to the rules could be made in their case: the amnesty proclamation did not apply to prisoners of war, and the Louisianans were in no way distinguished from other prisoners who wished to take the oath of allegiance.

Noble next applied to the generals who had been in charge of operations at Vicksburg. Had any promises been made to the Louisianans? Major General John A. Logan had made none; General Sherman said that Grant must know about the matter if anyone did; Grant replied that he had made no pledges, but recommended on September 22 that all prisoners sent north from Vicksburg after its capture be allowed to take the oath of allegiance and be set at liberty.

An order for their release was given on November 25. As soon as the prisoners' rolls were forwarded, the oath of allegiance was administered to over four hundred and fifty men and they were released on January 2 and 3, 1865. After eighteen months of confinement they were a worn, ragged, sorry crew, most of them without funds; the *Sentinel,* indignant at their long, undeserved imprisonment, demanded that they be given care and assistance in making their way home. The prisoners themselves showed a generous spirit, acknowledging with gratitude the efforts that had been made on their behalf by camp and state officials.[38]

February, 1865, was a month the prisoners had several reasons to remember. On the first of the month the rations of nonworking prisoners were cut again. The issue of hard bread was reduced from 14 to 10 ounces, but this reduction did not cause much additional discomfort at Camp Morton where prisoners received fresh bread from the post baker. The soap ration was reduced one half, the salt issue almost that much, and the vinegar ration was cut one third. The new regulations provided that these three items, if insufficient, might be increased by the commanding officer of the post not to exceed the ration allowed soldiers of the Union Army. Antiscorbutics were to be purchased from the prison fund if post surgeon and commandant certified that they were necessary. It is possible that Stevens and Surgeon Kipp, influenced by the heavy fatalities during the winter months, took advantage of these provisos to keep the rations of salt, vinegar, and vegetables at an adequate figure. About the middle of the month, after a complaint from the Confederate agent of exchange, camp sutlers were again permitted to sell vegetables; other foods and necessary clothing were allowed by a later order.[39]

The cut in the soap ration was less distressing at the moment. In December Lieutenant Davidson had found the men throwing their soap around the barracks. It was a sorry spectacle to be witnessed by the man who had expended much energy in improving the sanitary condition of barracks and prisoners, but common humanity forbade his compelling them to continue their outdoor bathing and laundry in icy weather.[40]

In the middle of the month Governor Morton adjourned

[38]*Official Records,* 2 series, VII, 466-67, 520, 608-10, 1158, 1179, 1232; Indianapolis *Sentinel,* January 4, 1865, p. 3, c. 2. Lefebvre and a companion made a table and box for Mrs. Stevens, as a token of their appreciation of Colonel Stevens' kindness. Carnahan, *Camp Morton,* 17.

[39]*Official Records,* 2 series, VIII, 62-63, 113, 144, 187-88, 209-10, 215, 310, 358, 412, 506. A district special order of August 2, 1864, required that bread for all the camps in and around Indianapolis be furnished from the post bakehouse. Mereness Calendar, War Department, Northern Department Orders, Vol. 80, p. 82.

[40]*Official Records,* 2 series, VII, 1273.

the legislature for a morning and led the members out to Camp Morton to see how the rebels fared. The prisoners behaved much better than on the inauspicious occasion when the Governor had introduced Parson Brownlow, standing quietly in line with uncovered heads while the procession passed by. Their uniforms were a faded motley of Confederate gray and Union blue, with blankets serving as coats in many cases, but according to the *Journal* most of the men appeared to be comfortably clothed and sufficiently fed. The new hospital quarters made a good impression.[41]

Far more momentous than legislative inspections and ration cuts was the knowledge that exchange of prisoners had recommenced and that Stevens had been ordered to make preparations for it. Increasing clamor among the citizens and a flood of petitions from the wretched Union men in the Andersonville, Macon, Charleston, and Savannah prison camps had forced the hands of Stanton and Grant, who believed that one way to shorten the war was to hang on to all Confederate prisoners. Grant put the matter realistically in a letter of August 18, 1864:[42]

"It is hard on our men held in Southern prisons not to exchange them, but it is humanity to those left in the ranks to fight our battles. Every man we hold, when released on parole or otherwise, becomes an active soldier against us at once either directly or indirectly. If we commence a system of exchange which liberates all prisoners taken, we will have to fight on until the whole South is exterminated."

Butler, then in charge of exchange, had the happy idea of exchanging invalids who would not be ready for the field in less than sixty days. This would fit in with Grant's ideas and at the same time quiet the public anger to some degree. Hoffman informed camp commandants of this plan on October 1, and directed them to be ready for the order to send sick prisoners forward. Some exchanges of this sort took place in the East during the autumn, but no men were sent from Camp Morton.[43]

[41] Indiana *House Journal*, 1865, p. 415; *Senate Journal*, 1865, p. 341; Indianapolis *Journal*, February 16, 1865, p. 1, c. 1.
[42] *Official Records*, 2 series, VII, 606-7.
[43] *Ibid.*, VII, 793, 907.

On the fifteenth of October Grant took over the business of exchange. Pressed by insistent citizens and a harrassed Congress, he began negotiations for the exchange of all prisoners, and on February 2, 1865, ordered his agent, Colonel John E. Mulford, to arrange for the delivery of three thousand a week. To delay the reinforcement of the Confederate armies by returning prisoners, he asked that disabled troops from the states of Missouri, Kentucky, Arkansas, Tennessee, and Louisiana—all now under Federal control—be sent first.[44] This part of the order immediately produced a new problem: a large proportion of the prisoners from the conquered states did not want to be exchanged.

At Camp Morton, for example, Stevens discovered that out of the 1,882 prisoners from Missouri, Kentucky, Tennessee, Arkansas, and Louisiana—about 45 per cent of the whole number of prisoners in camp—only 366 wanted to be exchanged. "The remaining 1,516," reported Stevens, "express freely their desire to remain in prison until such time as they can be released by taking the oath as prescribed in the President's proclamation, December 8, 1863." They were heartily sick of war; their states were out of the struggle; and most of them wanted nothing but a chance to rejoin their families and begin life over. Grant would have sent them on, but the Secretary of War directed that they be held at the camp until further orders.[45]

The two thousand prisoners who left Camp Morton for exchange in February and March, were, then, men who were eager to be back in the Confederate lines, though a large number of them were unfit for immediate service. In one installment of five hundred, two hundred were convalescents—the *Sentinel* predicted gloomily that many of them would never reach their destination. The first lot started off on February 19, in charge of a lieutenant and a hundred men. Cooked rations were supplied for four days. They were taken by

[44]*Official Records*, 2 series, VIII, 97-98, 170.
[45]Indianapolis *Journal*, February 8, 1865, p. 4, c. 1; February 11, p. 4, c. 1; *Official Records*, 2 series, VIII, 203. On February 24, Hoffman notified all camp commandants that no prisoners were to be sent for exchange who did not wish to go. *Ibid.*, VIII, 301.

rail to Baltimore, then by boat to Point Lookout, and from there to Aiken's Landing on the James River, where they were turned over to the Confederate agents about the first of March.[46] Five hundred more left for City Point, Virginia, about February 25, and in March another thousand were sent forward in two divisions. Among them were a few citizen prisoners whose homes were within the rebel lines. Citizens held on grave charges, or undergoing sentence were detained at the camp.[47]

Captain Castleman and Lieutenant Munford were sent forward at this time on special exchange. They reached Point Lookout, only to be detained on the strength of a letter from General Hovey, who considered Castleman too dangerous to be released and recommended that he be tried or banished. After several weeks of uncertainty and a sojourn in the Old Capital Prison at Washington they were returned to Indianapolis. On June 28, Castleman gave his parole to leave the country forever; he was put across the river into Canada at Detroit a few days later and lived abroad until pardoned by President Johnson. Munford was finally allowed to take the oath of allegiance and released.[48]

During February and March six hundred Confederates were released in addition to the number who were sent for exchange. Some of them belonged to the large number of prisoners who had refused parole at Vicksburg in 1863, and whose release on taking the oath of allegiance had been ordered some months before.[49] The rest—enough to make up two

[46]Mereness Calendar, Post Special Orders 12, 14, 16, and 19, Camp Morton, Indiana, February 17 and 25, March 4 and 14, 1865, War Department, Northern Department Orders, Vol. 126, pp. 54, 55, 56, 59; Wyeth, "Cold Cheer at Camp Morton," in *Century Magazine*, XLI, 852; Carnahan, *Camp Morton*, 59; Indianapolis *Sentinel*, February 23, 1865, p. 3, c. 1; February 27, p. 3, c. 1; March 16, p. 3, c. 1.

[47]*Official Records*, 2 series, VIII, 329.

[48]Castleman, *Active Service*, 180-88; *Official Records*, 2 series, VIII, 368-69, 477, 519, 704-5; Stevens to Hoffman, March 23, 1865, Hoffman to Stevens, March 24, 1865, Mereness Calendar, War Department, Letters Received, Secretary of War; Hovey to S. C. Skinner, June 28, 1865, *ibid.*, War Department, Northern Department Letter Books, Vol. 70, p. 105.

[49]*Official Records*, 2 series, VII, 1158.

companies—enlisted in the Union Army and were transferred to duty at Camp Douglas, Chicago.[50]

On the first of April, 1865, there remained at Camp Morton 1,408 prisoners. Lee's surrender on the ninth, removing the last possibility of a victory for the Confederacy, wiped out Grant's objections to releasing them. There remained the problem of getting them back to their homes in as orderly a fashion as possible. Preference was given those who had refused exchange and signified their willingness to take the oath of allegiance before the capture of Richmond. Camp commandants administered the oath and the discharged prisoners were furnished transportation home.[51]

Camp Morton was almost depopulated by the end of May. Day after day Stevens discharged groups of from forty to three or four hundred Confederates, until by June 1 there were only 308 prisoners left in camp. Many of the ragged and penniless Southerners made applications for work as soon as they were released.[52]

A General Order of June 6 provided for the release of prisoners who had not been included in any former order. Commanders were instructed to begin discharges with the men who had been longest in prison and those who were furthest from their homes. The oath of allegiance was required of all; those who wished to, were permitted to take the oath of amnesty.[53]

The last group departed from Indianapolis as several Indiana regiments returned to the jubilant and lavish welcome

[50]General Hovey had recommended the enlistment of prisoners of war at Camp Morton in September, 1864. Mereness Calendar, War Department, Northern Department Letter Books, Vol. 69, pp. 138-39. An order for the enlistment of two companies was given on March 14, 1865. *Ibid.,* War Department, Northern Department Orders, Vol. 84, pp. 22, 24-25; Vol. 126, p. 61.

[51]General Orders No. 85, May 8, 1865, *Official Records, 2* series, VIII, 538. This order excepted all officers above the rank of colonel.

[52]Mereness Calendar, Post Special Orders, May 10, 1865 and following, War Department, Northern Department Orders, Vol. 126, pp. 67 ff.; Indianapolis *Sentinel,* May 12, 1865, p. 3, c. 1; May 22, p. 3, c. 1; May 23, p. 3, c. 1.

[53]*Official Records, 2* series, VIII, 641. Officers above the rank of captain and graduates of the United States Naval or Military academies were excepted.

of a happy state. No one could look upon the two groups of men and remain untouched by the contrast between them. "Yesterday . . . the last remnant of the rebel prisoners confined in Camp Morton were released," said the *Journal* of June 14. "In tattered gray and butternut the poor fellows straggled down our streets in search of transportation to their homes. The departure of many of these has been delayed because they were in the hospital. As we saw them, haggard and pale, tottering along with their little poverty-stricken bundles, we felt sincerely sorry for them. In our heart there was no bitterness of feeling against them; and we were glad, without qualification, that they were free once more.

". . . They go back to a conquered country—to overgrown fields—to ruined villages—to homes, the chimneys of which only are left. This could not be helped. War is a hard thing, and it leaves a black and damning trail."[54]

In the military prison at Camp Morton there remained seven unhappy men who should have been sharing the welcome given the Union troops. They had deserted from the Union Army, and while prisoners in the hands of the enemy had taken the oath of allegiance to the Confederate Government and joined the rebel forces. When chance made them prisoners of their former comrades they were conveyed to the Camp Morton jail.

Now that the war was over, officials were eager to get them off their hands as quietly as possible. No one wanted an expensive and embarrassing trial, and the men could do no harm if released. Like the other prisoners they were given the oath of allegiance and set free. Forty members of the Veteran Reserve Corps who had been consigned to the guardhouse for mutiny were disposed of with the same regard for peace and economy: they were given a dishonorable discharge without pay.[55]

Left in Greenlawn Cemetery were the bodies of the Confederates who had died at Camp Morton since February, 1862. Some of the bodies were later exhumed and returned to relatives in the South; most of them remained in the little

[54]Indianapolis *Journal,* June 14, 1865, p. 2, c. 1.
[55]*Official Records,* 2 series, VIII, 691-92, 704-5.

cemetery, the long ranges of graves slowly disappearing under a growth of high grass, the painted identification numbers on the wooden headboards fading into undecipherable blurs. In the sixties, the old City Cemetery and Greenlawn ceased to be used as public burial places, and industrial developments began to encroach upon the site. Occasional inquiries were made by officers of Confederate associations as to the condition of the prisoners' graves, but nothing was done about renumbering them or improving their condition.

In the 1870's the Vandalia Railroad, needing part of the ground for an engine house and additional tracks, exchanged some property on the west side of the cemetery for ground on the north line in which there were two rows of graves. The bodies from these two rows were removed and reburied in two parallel trenches, but the new graves were not marked. In 1906 Colonel William Elliott, detailed by the War Department to locate the burial place of the Confederate dead, examined the area, and decided that a plot about forty-five feet wide by two hundred feet long near the present site of the Diamond Chain plant, was the place where the reinterments had been made in 1870. This space was enclosed by an iron fence, and in 1912, the Federal Government erected a monument there in honor of the Confederate prisoners buried at Greenlawn.

As growing industries of the section continued to press hard upon the memorial, the Southern Club of Indianapolis asked the Board of Park Commissioners for permission to remove the monument to Garfield Park. In 1928 it was removed to its present position in the southern section of the park. The names and organizations of the dead are listed on bronze tablets; the shaft bears the following inscription:

PAX

Erected
by the
United States
to mark
The Burial Place
of 1616 Confederate
Soldiers and Sailors
Who died Here
While Prisoners
of War
And Whose Graves
Cannot Now be
Identified

The plot enclosed after Colonel Elliott's investigation is now overgrown with weeds and grass, earth has been filled in and the fence removed. An old resident who said he had witnessed the reinterment of bodies made in 1870, believed that it was made at least a hundred yards southwest of the plot designated by Colonel Elliott, but it has been proved that there were some burials in the enclosed area, and in 1931 the War Department had them removed to Crown Hill Cemetery. They are buried along the north side of Section 32 and the place is marked by a dignified stone monument.[56]

At Camp Morton, disposal of camp property began as soon as the prisoners were gone. Property that had been purchased from the prisoners' fund was appraised and sold at public auction in July, 1865, and on August 2 the buildings were declared vacant. Claims of the State Board of Agriculture for damages

[56]Indianapolis *Sentinel,* January 31, 1865, p. 3, c. 1; Indianapolis *News,* February 24, 1897, p. 6, c. 3; November 29, 1906, p. 5, c. 2; p. 6, c. 3; Report of Fifth Corps Area Inspector to the Inspector General, February 17, 1931; interview with the late David I. McCormick; Crown Hill Cemetery Records; Transcript of the Grave Stones Remaining in Greenlawn Cemetery, Indianapolis, 1920, compiled under the supervision of Joseph R. H. Moore, and presented to the Indiana State Library.

to the fairgrounds were eventually settled by the United States for $9,816.56.[57]

There was little about the Camp Morton of midsummer, 1865, to recall Henderson's Grove or the fairgrounds of 1861. Hundreds of trees had been cut for lumber or firewood, and the earth was pitted and scarred. Three thousand dollars was voted by the city for its rehabilitation. Later an "exposition building" was erected, and the grounds were used by the fair association until the nineties. Under the pressure of a growing population, the property was sold, the state ditch was supplanted by a part of the city's drainage system, streets were built, and the area was platted as a residence district which is still known as Morton Place.[58]

Between 1913 and 1915 two or three different groups and organizations made tentative plans to mark the site of Camp Morton, but for some reason none of these was carried out. In 1916 the teachers and pupils of School Forty-five (at Park Avenue and Twenty-third Street) marked the camp site by a boulder placed at Alabama and Nineteenth streets where the main entrance to the enclosure probably lay.[59] Cut into the stone is the following inscription:

CAMP MORTON
1861-1865
ERECTED BY SCHOOL FORTY-FIVE
1916

[57]Mereness Calendar, Post Orders 6 and 10, Camp Morton, June 28 and July 15, 1865, War Department, Northern Department Orders, Vol. 126, pp. 111, 114; *Official Records,* 2 series, VIII, 714; State Board of Agriculture, *Report,* 1868, p. 29.

[58]Brown, "History of Indianapolis," in *Logan's Indianapolis Directory . . . 1868,* p. 64; deed of December 22, 1891, Deed Book 25, p. 243, Marion County Courthouse

[59]Indianapolis *News,* August 15, 1913; January 16, 1915; May 31, 1916; Indianapolis *Star,* August 29, 1914.

APPENDIX

APPENDIX

I. ABSTRACT OF MONTHLY RETURNS FROM CAMP MORTON[1]

Date	On hand	Joined	Total	Transferred		Died	Escaped	Released	Total loss	Sick	Citizen
				Other stations	Exchanged						
1862 July	4,018	198	4,216	...	...	21	5	...	26	120	...
Aug.	4,190	64	4,254	4,122	...	26	...	...	4,148	103	...
Sept.	103	...	103	...	98	3	...	2	103	...	...
1863 July	111	1,165	1,276	6	...	16	2	...	24	39	3
Aug.	1,252	1,808	3,060	1,142	...	26	6	336	1,510	98	13
Sept.	1,550	51	1,601	2	...	23	19	70	114	111	24
Oct.	1,487	1,035	2,522	21	...	36	10	7	74	261	37
Nov.	2,448	706	3,154	...	...	68	2	9	79	328	29
Dec.	3,075	297	3,372	...	5	91	...	3	99	244	33
1864 Jan.	3,273	6	3,279	13	...	104	3	1	121	251	33
Feb.	3,158	57	3,215	...	...	69	18	7	94	326	32
Mar.	3,121	1	3,122	500	...	49	...	3	552	271	29
Apr.	2,570	93	2,663	...	...	19	1	43	63	235	26
May	2,600	609	3,209	...	...	17	2	4	23	248	40
June	3,186	1,350	4,536	55	...	34	...	16	105	324	38
July	4,431	568	4,999	...	4	81	...	8	93	350	35
Aug.	4,906	43	4,949	4	...	91	7	8	110	341	33
Sept.	4,839	...	4,839	8	...	33	6	14	61	293	32
Oct.	4,778	3	4,781	...	...	21	1	12	34	217	31
Nov.	4,747	5	4,752	...	1	18	31	24	74	205	29
Dec.	4,678	167	4,845	16	...	53	...	39	108	354	26
1865 Jan.	4,737	51	4,788	...	...	117	...	472	589	355	24
Feb.	4,199	16	4,215	...	1,000	133	2	214	1,349	272	19
Mar.	2,866	2	2,868	2	1,000	70	...	388	1,460	218	6
Apr.	1,408	...	1,408	9	...	10	...	45	64	190	2
May	1,343	23	1,366	...	...	10	...	1,037	1,047	46	16
June	319	...	319	...	...	2	2	308	312	...	13
July	7	...	7	...	...	...	...	7	...	...	...

[1]Adapted from tables covering eleven prison camps, *Official Records*, 2 series, VIII, 987-1003.

II. DEATHS FROM CERTAIN DISEASES AND CLASSES OF DISEASES AT CAMP MORTON, JUNE, 1863-JUNE, 1865.[1]

Number of months recorded 25

Mean strength present 2,865

	Cases	Deaths
All diseases and injuries	9,122	1,187
Wounds, injuries and unspecified diseases	259	12
Specified diseases	8,863	1,175
Continued Fevers	55	42
Malarial Fevers	1,954	119
Eruptive Fevers	548	85
Diarrhea and Dysentery	2,241	315
Anemia	68	4
Consumption	34	26
Rheumatism	190	5
Scurvy	778	6
Bronchitis	178	1
Pneumonia and Pleurisy	1,351	495
Other diseases	1,466	77
Total specified diseases	8,863	1,175

[1]Adapted from Table XVIII, covering nine prison depots, in *Medical and Surgical History of the War*, Medical Volume, pt. III, 46.

III. RATION REDUCTIONS, 1864-65

	April 1864[1]	June 1864[2] nonworkers	June 1864[2] workers	January 1865[3] nonworkers	January 1865[3] workers
Hard bread or	14 oz.	14 oz.	12 oz.	10 oz.	12 oz.
Soft bread or	18 oz.	16 oz.	18 oz.	16 oz.	18 oz.
Corn meal	18 oz.	16 oz.	18 oz.	16 oz.	18 oz.
Beef or	14 oz.	14 oz.	16 oz.	14 oz.	16 oz.
Bacon, pork	10 oz.	10 oz.	12 oz.	10 oz.	12 oz.
Beans, peas or	6 qts. (100 men)	12½ lbs.	14 lbs.	12½ lbs.	15 lbs.
Hominy, rice	8 lbs.	8 lbs.	10 lbs.	8 lbs.	10 lbs.
Sugar	14 lbs.	12 lbs. ⎫ sick &	12 lbs.	12 lbs. ⎫ sick &	12 lbs.
Coffee, raw or	7 lbs.	7 lbs. ⎬ wounded	7 lbs.	7 lbs. ⎬ wounded	7 lbs.
ground	5 lbs.	5 lbs. ⎪ only; al-	5 lbs.	5 lbs. ⎪ only; al-	5 lbs.
Tea	18 oz.	16 oz. ⎭ ternate days	16 oz.	16 oz. ⎭ ternate days	16 oz.
Soap	4 lbs.	4 lbs.	4 lbs.	2 lbs.	4 lbs.
Candles, tallow	6 lbs.	—	—	—	—
adamantine	5 lbs.	—	—	—	—
Salt	2 qts.	3¾ lbs.	3¾ lbs.	2 lbs.	3¾ lbs.
Molasses	1 qt.	—	—	—	—
Vinegar	3 qts.	3 qts.	3 qts.	2 qts.	3 qts.
Potatoes	30 lbs.	15 lbs.	—	—	—

[1] *Official Records*, 2 series, VII, 73.

[2] *Ibid.*, VII, 183, 367.

[3] *Ibid.*, VIII, 62. Desiccated compressed potatoes, or desiccated compressed mixed vegetables might be substituted for beans, peas, rice, or hominy. The ration of soap, salt, or vinegar, if insufficient, was subject to increase, by order of the post commandant, not to exceed the ration allowed to Union troops.

IV. ABSTRACT OF SUBSISTENCE STORES ISSUED TO REB.
CAPTAIN L. L. MOORE AN

		RATIONS OF							
Average number of prisoners	1864	Pork.	Bacon.	Salt Beef.	Fresh Beef.	Flour.	Hard Bread.	Corn Meal.	Beans
2,918	Jan.	2,148	35,066		51,056	88,180	26,332		7,
2,861	Feb.		28,971		51,850	{ 310 bbls., 86 lbs.	35,856		12,
2,552	Mar.	{ 5 bbls., 20 lbs.	30,829		47,825	{ 466 bbls., 38 lbs.	14,239		11,
2,252	Apr.	{ 16 bbls., 138 lbs.	21,991		42,237	{ 473 bbls., 188 lbs.			10,
2,550	May		32,299		24,369	{ 414 bbls., 46 lbs.	6,439		3,
3,201	June		29,629		42,560	{ 411 bbls., 3 lbs.	13,557		3,
4,455	July		38,823		66,516	{ 498 bbls., 163 lbs.	34,978	384	6,
4,432	Aug.	{ 12 bbls., 102 lbs.	16,918		93,030	{ 578 bbls., 43 lbs.	8,319	14,554	5,
4,356	Sep.		12,195		97,276	{ 624 bbls., 26 lbs.	7,312	35,273	5,
4,383	Oct.		12,833		100,944	{ 448 bbls., 24 lbs.	11,192		8,
4,368	Nov.	149 lbs.	2,318		111,221	{ 579 bbls., 67 lbs.	15,317		8,
4,315	Dec.	24 lbs.	927	11,473	97,763	{ 595 bbls., 15 lbs.	14,998		8,
Total		Lbs. 13,957	Lbs. 262,799	Lbs. 11,473	Lbs. 826,447	1,146,540	Lbs. 188,533	Lbs. 50,216	Lb 91,

CAMP MORTON

PRISONERS AT CAMP MORTON DURING THE YEAR 1864, BY CAPTAIN NAT. SHURTLEFF, A. C. S.[1]

RATIONS OF

Potatoes.	Rice.	Hominy.	Coffee, Roasted.	Tea.	Sugar.	Vinegar.	Candles, Adamantine.	Soap.	Salt.	Pepper, Black.	Molasses.
5,238	2,926	875	4,437	526	13,569	904	1,131	3,619	3,392	226	226
13,110	5,524	2,487	4,873	288	12,016	801	1,001	3,204	3,004	200	201
23,768	4,870	3,052	5,840	116	12,109	792	990	3,169	2,971	178	198
20,268	4,058	2,698	5,405		10,134	675	844	2,702	2,534	169	168
23,858	2,077	2,083	5,037	79	11,134	795	662	3,181	2,783	199	198
14,407	2,565	2,561	584		1,635	720	97	3,842	3,602		29
	3,572	8,570				136		5,525	5,180		
	3,962	3,544				1,230		5,496	5,152		
	3,484	3,485				980		5,228	4,901		
	1,047	4,208				1,019		5,436	5,096		
		5,157				983		5,242	4,915		
		5,181				1,003		5,351	517		
Lbs. 100,649	Lbs. 34,805	Lbs. 38,901	Lbs. 26,176	Lbs. 1,009	Lbs. 60,597	Gals. 10,738	Lbs. 4,725	Lbs. 57,996	Lbs. 48,547	Lbs. 972	Gals. 1,020

[1]Adapted from a table printed in Carnahan, Camp Morton, pp. 54-55.